THE
LINCOLN
HIGHWAY
IN IOWA

A HISTORY

DARCY DOUGHERTY MAULSBY

THE
History
PRESS

Published by The History Press
Charleston, SC
www.historypress.com

Front cover images: The famed Lincoln Highway has been called the "Main Street Across America," and it has played a vital part in Iowa history for more than a century. If you've ever driven on an interstate, you owe a debt of gratitude to the Lincoln Highway, the first coast-to-coast, improved highway across the United States. Today, you can explore the Lincoln Highway Heritage Byway. As it is Iowa's longest and most historic byway, you'll travel through more than 460 miles of history, recreation and welcoming Iowa communities. Along your Lincoln Highway journey, you'll encounter (*clockwise from top right*) a Mount Vernon–area barn featuring Grant Wood's iconic *American Gothic*; delectable pies at the Lincoln Café in Belle Plaine; the historic Moss markers north of Scranton; quirky sights like Abraham Lincoln carved into an old tree trunk in Nevada; and the classic Youngville Café, a one-stop roadside business in rural Benton County.

Back cover images: The national Lincoln Highway Association met in Denison in the summer of 2017, which is why this classic auto was parked outside the historic Cronk's restaurant. For generations, one of most recognizable landmarks along the Lincoln Highway in Iowa has been this 1915 bridge near Tama.

First published 2022

Manufactured in the United States

ISBN 9781467149808

Library of Congress Control Number: 2022939461

Notice: The information in this book is true and complete to the best of our knowledge. It is offered without guarantee on the part of the author or The History Press. The author and The History Press disclaim all liability in connection with the use of this book.

CONTENTS

ACKNOWLEDGEMENTS

P eople sometimes ask me how I find the stories I tell. Well, I ask a lot of questions; I tap into my network and rely on people who are willing to listen to me when I reach out by e-mail or phone to say, "This is Darcy Maulsby, and I'm a writer from Lake City who's working on a book. Would you be willing to visit with me?"

I'm grateful for all the people who've said yes to this book, including the Clinton County Historical Society, the innkeepers at the Lincoln Hotel in Lowden, Cedar Rapids native Roz Schultes, Mary Evans (for her knowledge of the Mount Vernon and Lisbon area), volunteers at the Youngville Café and the new friends I met in Belle Plaine, including City Manager Stephen Beck, Bill Sankot, Mitch Malcolm and Mary Helen Preston. I also appreciated Jodi Philipp's hospitality when I attended a murder-mystery dinner at her Periwinkle Place Manor in Chelsea.

Thank you to the Le Grand Pioneer Heritage Library for introducing me to a whole chapter of Iowa's ancient history and fossils—fascinating! I appreciated Sandy Taylor Short's hospitality in Marshalltown a few years ago when she treated me to a great meal at Taylor's Maid-Rite. Then there's Sandra Huemann-Kelly, who helped me not only when she ran Niland's Café in Colo but also anytime I had Lincoln Highway questions. Thank you, also, to the Ames History Museum for sharing some fascinating vintage photos.

In Greene County, I'm grateful to Roger Aegerter and the Greene County Historical Society, as well as Lincoln Highway legends Bob and

Joyce Ausberger. Talk about people who have worked tirelessly to keep the history alive! Then there are the great volunteers at the Dow House in Dow City and the Donna Reed Theatre in Denison—people who maintain these beautiful, historic properties so others can experience this history in person.

Then there are the Arcadia-area folks (including Laurie Blum, the FAC Cooperative team and Dan Julin at Arcadia Meats); Jill Schaben and Jim Schaben in Dunlap; the incredible folks in Woodbine, including Deb Sprecker, executive director of Woodbine Main Street; Jeff and Nikki Davis of Building Grounds and Heavy Metal Renaissance; and Todd Waite and the fun team at Good Fellows.

I can't forget Susan Cates from JC's Dairy Den in Missouri Valley, Dale Schmidt from Henry's Diner in Crescent, the amazing Donna Malone from the Pink Poodle Steakhouse in Crescent, Dan and Kathy Poulos (who are living proof of the American dream), Richard Warner with the Historical Society of Pottawattamie County (for patiently answering all types of questions) and Kat Slaughter and Sergeant Jason LeMaster for all their information about the Squirrel Cage Jail in Council Bluffs.

Thanks to Shadric Smith, too, for writing "Rollin' Down that Lincoln Highway," a song I listened to often as I wrote this book. I also owe a debt of gratitude to the writers and historians, including Drake Hokanson and Brian Butko, who were interested in the Lincoln History long before me and have been willing to share their insights with me.

I know I haven't thanked everyone who contributed to this book, but rest assured, I do value you. Finally, I'd like to thank Chad Rhoad and the great team at The History Press for helping bring this book to life so we can all take a journey along the ever-fascinating Lincoln Highway in Iowa.

INTRODUCTION

Have you ever traveled on an interstate? If so, you owe a debt of gratitude to the Lincoln Highway. I get two types of reactions when I start talking about this remarkable piece of Iowa and American history. Older folks tend to nod in agreement, saying that they've heard of the Lincoln Highway, although many admit they don't know much about it. With younger people, I tend to get a blank stare, sometimes followed by, "Huh?"

Sometimes people ask me why I care about the Lincoln Highway. I didn't grow up in a Lincoln Highway community, nor do I live in one now. I do live about twenty miles north of the Lincoln Highway, however, and have for most of my life. I've traveled on many parts of the Lincoln Highway years before I'd heard of the highway or its history.

You see, I've been an ag journalist for twenty-six years and have traveled millions of miles on the back roads of Iowa and other parts of rural America. I'm also eternally curious. I pay attention to the world around me and never stop asking why. I always wondered why those mysterious white monuments were located north of Scranton with the words "Moss" on them, topped with a bust of Abraham Lincoln. I wondered about the old grain elevator with an artistic cornstalk on it in Woodbine. What stories could they tell?

As my job took me across the state, I started paying attention to the red, white and blue Lincoln Highway signs and Lincoln Highway Heritage Byway signs I noticed. I began researching online to learn more about the Lincoln Highway. I started reading books about this famous "Main Street Across America." There was just one problem. While there's a wealth of information about the Lincoln Highway as a whole, from New York to California, I felt like Iowa got the short end of the stick. Where were the in-depth stories about the landmarks and interesting side notes I was seeing in my travels along the Lincoln Highway?

That's when you know it's time to write a book. So here it is. Please join me on a virtual journey to recall a time when the Lincoln Highway was new, discover how it evolved and explore what it looks like today. We can do this because as much as 85 percent of the original highway is still drivable in the Hawkeye State, as the Lincoln Highway Association noted.

To me, this is why no state can compare to Iowa when it comes to getting a sense of what it might have been like for earlier generations of motorists on the Lincoln Highway. In some cases, like the Lincoln Hotel in Lowden, we can stay overnight the same place weary travelers did more than one hundred years ago. We can eat in the same cafés, like the Lincoln Café in Belle Plaine, Taylor's Maid-Rite in Marshalltown or the Pink Poodle Steakhouse in Crescent, where folks have enjoyed homemade comfort food for decades.

There are countless pieces of the past just waiting to be discovered along the Lincoln Highway in Iowa, and oh the people we'll meet! This reminds me of the late Charles Kuralt. After he retired from a thirty-seven-year career as a reporter for CBS News, he hit the road to see the real America. Kuralt was not in search of crises or epiphanies. He valued good food, neighborliness, craftsmanship, quaintness and quirkiness, all linked to the good, decent people who still live in America's cities, small towns and farms. You'll find these types of stories here, along our Lincoln Highway journey in Iowa.

One more thing—I came across a 2004 Associated Press article detailing how three graduate students were dispatched across the Lincoln Highway in the summer of 2002 to document the historic features (motels, gas stations, bridges and other landmarks) along the way, from New York to San Francisco. "They had eight weeks...on the backest road possible," said Kevin Patrick, a geography professor at Indiana University of Pennsylvania.

If this is the "backest" back road possible, I'm all in. Those grad students in 2002 identified 147 significant features of the Lincoln Highway in Iowa, and this book will give you a glimpse into many of them. While this book isn't intended to help you follow the exact route of the original Lincoln Highway (there are other books much better suited to that), and not all the people and places in this book are located exactly on the Lincoln Highway, all give richer insights into Iowa's Lincoln Highway heritage.

Let me be your guide on this unforgettable journey. I hope you enjoy the ride.

GETTING IOWA OUT OF THE MUD

T he dawn of the twentieth century ushered in an exciting new era of seemingly unlimited potential in Iowa and the wider world, thanks to the wonders of modern technology. Electricity was illuminating towns and cities, airplanes were taking flight and a thrilling new invention, the automobile, was capturing the imagination of Americans from coast to coast.

While automobiles were once considered expensive toys for the rich, they were becoming more common, as countless car manufacturing companies sprang up across the nation. Nothing accelerated this trend, however, like the 1908 debut of Henry Ford's revolutionary Model T. Soon thousands of Model Ts were rolling off the assembly line in Michigan each year, spurred by Americans' seemingly insatiable demand for this simple, affordable car.

Iowans embraced autos with gusto within a few short years. In 1905, only 799 motor vehicles were registered in Iowa, according to the article "Getting Out of the Mud," by George S. May, which appeared in the January 1955 edition of *The Palimpsest*. By 1915, however, the figure had leaped to 147,078. (By 2015, the total number of vehicles registered in Iowa—including autos, buses, trucks, trailers, etc.—equaled 4,341,801, according to the Iowa Department of Transportation. What a difference ninety or one hundred years can make!)

Iowa wouldn't have millions of vehicles on the road today, however, if roads hadn't been improved a century ago. While it's hard to imagine now,

In the 1910s, most roads in Iowa were just dirt. They were bumpy and dusty in dry weather and impassable in wet weather when they turned to mud, as this driver near Tama was well aware. To get from one place to another, it was much easier to take the train. *Courtesy of Lincoln Highway Museum.*

there were almost no good roads to speak of in the United States, especially in Iowa, as late as 1912. Most roads were just dirt—bumpy and dusty in dry weather, impassable in wet weather. To get from one place to another, it was much easier to take the train.

Yet a growing number of motorists (or daredevils, depending on your point of view) had no interest in waiting for the train and its schedules. Thanks to a whim and a $50 bet (worth roughly $1,600 in today's money), Horatio Nelson Jackson, a thirty-one-year-old physician from Burlington, Vermont, drove a 1903, twenty-horsepower, cherry red Winton touring car from San Francisco, California, to New York City from May to July 1903, often on roads that were primitive at best. Accompanied by his mechanic, Sewall Crocker, and a bulldog named Bud that they picked up along the way, Jackson broke the cross-country barrier through sheer determination and perseverance. The trip took sixty-three days, including numerous delays while the two men waited for parts or paused to hoist the Winton up and over gullies and other obstacles. Still, they won the $50 bet by arriving in New York City less than ninety days after they started.

George A. Wyman made a cross-country motorcycle journey in the summer of 1903. As he passed through Iowa, he generally followed the route that would become the Lincoln Highway a decade later. A number of Lincoln Highway towns mark these waypoints. This signage is outside the Donna Reed Theatre in downtown Denison. *Author's collection.*

Then there was George A. Wyman, who made a similar cross-country journey that summer of 1903 on a motorcycle. Wyman started in San Francisco on May 16 and arrived in New York City on July 6, 1903. He rode a 200cc, 1.25-horsepower "California" motorcycle, which he often referred to as a "bicycle" in his journal. "The June floods had preceded me surely enough, and the roads were so muddy that I could hardly force the bicycle along," he wrote as he slogged along from Council Bluffs to Denison—the future route of the Lincoln Highway. "I took a snapshot of my bicycle in one place where it was kept upright by the mud."

Sometimes the sloppy roads hurled him off his motorcycle. "The mud along that part of the world is of the gumbo variety, that sticks like glue when it is moist and dries as hard and solid as bricks," Wyman wrote. "I held quite a good-sized tract of Iowa real estate when I arose, but I reflected that it was better to have landed in a soft spot than it would have been to have struck a place where the flinty ruts were sticking up 5 inches like cleavers with ragged edges."

Motorized vehicles crossing the Iowa countryside were a rare sight indeed at this time. "I met quite a number of wagons," Wyman wrote. "Motor vehicles of any sort are not common enough thereabouts as yet for the horses to be unafraid of them. Eight out of ten horses I met wanted to climb a telegraph pole or leap the fence at the sight and sound of my harmless little vehicle, and the farmers used language that would make a pirate blush."

Often, it was just easier to ride the motorcycle on the railroad tracks. "At Woodbine, I concluded to take to the railroad tracks to escape the affectionate hugging of the gumbo mud and the objurgations [sic] of the farmers, a number of whom told me I 'ought to keep that thing off the road altogether,'" Wyman wrote. "I went on the tracks of the Northwestern, and had not ridden far before I was ordered off by a section boss. This was the first time this thing happened to me, but it was not the last time."

After making a detour through the fields, Wyman returned to the tracks but was chased off a second time. He shifted his route to the tracks of the Illinois Central, which ran near the North Western's rails, and had no more trouble with section bosses. He reached Denison at 8:00 p.m., after covering only seventy-five miles in thirteen and a half hours. (That same trip would take about an hour and fifteen minutes today.)

Both Wyman and Jackson not only survived all these ordeals on their cross-country journeys but also were lauded for their accomplishments. Their achievements also changed the way Americans thought about long-distance travel. It now seemed possible—even desirable—to move about the country in cars instead of trains.

Those men's pioneering trips inspired an even more ambitious journey by 1908: the famed New York to Paris Auto Race. On the morning of February 12 (Lincoln's birthday), six cars from four different countries lined up in the swirling snow in Times Square, New York City, surrounded by a frenzied crowd of roughly 250,000 people. It was the start of a twenty-one-thousand-mile-course across three continents and six countries. The teams' estimated six-month trek would take them right across Iowa on a route that would foreshadow the Lincoln Highway.

The competitors drove a Sizaire-Naudin from France, a Protos from Germany, a Moto-Bloc from France, a De Dion from France, a Brixia-Zust from Italy and a Thomas Flyer car from the United States. "There would only be one—one race around the world, one start, and one particular way that, for the people who lived through it, the world would never be the same," wrote Julie Fenster in her book *Race of the Century: The Heroic True Story of the 1908 New York to Paris Auto Race*. "The automobile was about to take it all on…to the farthest reaches to which it could lead. On that absurdity, the auto was about to come of age."

Of course there were skeptics, but the editor of the *Denison Bulletin* wasn't one of them: "You think that automobile race doesn't amount to anything? Well, now, how much more have you thought about and studied autos the past few weeks than you ever did before? And what you have been doing, 50 million other people have been doing also, and of that 50 million, many have the money to spend for machines of their own. See?"

By the time the teams crossed the Mississippi River, Iowa's unimproved roads proved to be a nightmare for the competitors. It didn't help that the teams were trying to race through Iowa in March, as winter slowly turned to spring. When the Thomas Flyer raced into Boone, the car lurched sideways each time the vehicle hit a hole along the muddy roads. "One of my favorite quotes comes from George Schuster when he crossed Iowa during the 1908 New York-to-Paris race," said Brian Butko, author of the book *Greetings from the Lincoln Highway: A Road Trip Celebration of America's First Coast-to-Coast Highway*. "'We slid from one side of the road to the other. We covered more miles sidewise than ahead.'"

When Monty Roberts, Schuster's teammate, stopped the car for the night in Ogden, locals surrounded the car, shouting, "Speech! Speech!" Roberts was too tired for tact. "I don't like your roads. The mud is something awful. The hospitality of the people is splendid to behold, but your towpaths—."

In 1908, competitors from around the world sped across Iowa along the future route of the Lincoln Highway during the New York to Paris Auto Race. The German team drove this Protos vehicle, shown here in Marshalltown. Teams were often stuck in Iowa due to muddy roads and mechanical breakdowns. *Courtesy of Library of Congress.*

With that, he stopped talking, extricated himself from his mud-stiffened overcoat and headed into the Ogden House hotel to check in.

Other teams fared even worse. As the Zust plowed west, a wheel fell off the Italian car near Denison. The team lost two days to that wheel—and the mud. Team Zust had to walk the last few miles into Denison. "In fact, they did it several times, carrying loads of supplies from the car, which was overloaded and sinking in the mud," Fenster wrote. Antonio Scarfoglio had to convince his teammate Emilio Sirtori not to quit in Denison.

When the Italian team finally made it to Council Bluffs, the last stop in muddy Iowa, Sirtori was feeling better, in part because the Illinois Central Railroad allowed the team to drive on its tracks, with a special locomotive as an escort. They would not win the race, however. The American Thomas Flyer team was declared the winner in Paris, France, on July 30, 1908.

THE BIRTH OF THE LINCOLN HIGHWAY

As automobile fever spread, an entrepreneur named Carl Fisher took note. His Indianapolis Motor Speedway had proven to be a big success, especially after he paved it with brick and started the Indianapolis 500 in May 1911. By 1912, Fisher was dreaming of another grand idea: a highway spanning the continent from coast to coast.

"A road across the United States!" Fisher proclaimed when he hosted a large dinner party at the Old Deutsches Haus in Indianapolis in early September 1912 for leaders in the automobile industry. "Let's build it before we're too old to enjoy it!"

He called his idea the Coast-to-Coast Rock Highway. He estimated that the graveled road would cost about $10 million, low even for 1912. He wanted the highway finished in time so thousands of people could cross the continent from New York City to San Francisco, California, which was hosting the 1915 Panama-Pacific International Exposition, a world's fair designed to celebrate the completion of the Panama Canal and America's ascendancy to the global stage.

To fund the proposed coast-to-coast highway, Fisher asked for cash donations from auto manufacturers. The public could become members of the highway organization for $5. Fisher knew that success of the $10 million project would depend on the support of Henry Ford. Even after many persuasive attempts by friends and close associates, Ford refused to support the project. The public would never learn to fund good roads if private industry did it for them, he reasoned.

This put the proposed highway in jeopardy, but by now, enthusiasm had spread nationwide for the project. Fisher didn't give up. Neither did Frank Seiberling, founder of Goodyear Tire and Rubber Company, or Henry Joy, president of the Packard Motor Car Company. Joy came up with the idea of naming the highway after Abraham Lincoln. The name "Lincoln" captured Fisher's fancy, since he realized it would give great patriotic appeal to the highway. On July 1, 1913, the project was officially incorporated as the Lincoln Highway

Carl Fisher, who founded the Indianapolis Motor Speedway and Indianapolis 500, dreamed of another grand idea: a highway spanning the continent, from coast to coast. In 1912, he proposed the concept for what would become the Lincoln Highway. *Courtesy of Library of Congress.*

Association (LHA). Henry Joy was elected president, and Carl Fisher was elected vice-president.

Now it was time to select a route for the Lincoln Highway. As far as Joy was concerned, directness was the most important factor. By bypassing many scenic attractions and larger cities, narrow winding roadways and congestion could be avoided. Maybe it's not surprising that many well-established, older paths ended up beside or beneath the Lincoln Highway, including parts of the Oregon Trail and the Pony Express. Rail lines like the Chicago and North Western (which merged with the Union Pacific in 1995) would also parallel the new Lincoln Highway for many miles.

When the LHA announced its 3,389-mile route in September 14, 1913, the public learned it would start in Times Square in New York City and pass through New Jersey, Pennsylvania, Ohio, Indiana, Illinois, Iowa, Nebraska, Wyoming, Utah, Nevada and California, ending in Lincoln Park in San Francisco. Almost immediately, the LHA received letters trying to change the route; it politely declined every request.

The LHA dedicated the route of the Lincoln Highway on October 31, 1913. Bonfires and celebrations of all kinds marked ceremonies in hundreds of communities along the route, including many Lincoln Highway towns in Iowa. Lowden's newspaper editor spread the word: "A meeting will be held in every town along the Transcontinental Highway in Iowa on the night of October 31 to ratify the selection of it as the Lincoln Highway across the state. Every town from coast to coast has been requested to hold meetings, and as Lowden is in a very important position on the route, plans should be made by some of our road boosters for this meeting."

Lincoln Highway boosters nationwide also encouraged locals to mark the route. "At the encouragement of the Lincoln Highway Association, civic groups, business people and general citizenry from communities along the route fanned out to paint Lincoln Highway markers in patriotic red, white and blue stripes on barns, trees, rocks, telephone poles, and fence posts," explained author Drake Hokanson. "What the marking job lacked in standardization or neatness it made up in enthusiasm. Anybody lucky enough to live or do business along the Lincoln Highway was proud of that fact."

TRACING THE EVOLUTION OF A LEGENDARY HIGHWAY

To build support for the Lincoln Highway, the LHA designated a system of "consuls" in communities along the highway to serve as local ambassadors to represent the highway in local affairs. They would also assist visitors and inform the national LHA headquarters about matters concerning the highway.

In this era, however, there wasn't much of a highway to be concerned about. No improvements had been made to the Lincoln Highway. There were barely maps to guide travelers along the route. The long-distance motorist of this era was "a pathfinder in every sense of the word," wrote Drake Hokanson in his book *The Lincoln Highway: Main Street Across America.* "Gulf Oil wouldn't invent the free gas-station road map until 1913, and guides existed only for the eastern states. Stopping for local advice was of limited help. Motorists found that they had to stop every few miles to ask for directions; a farmer or resident seldom had any knowledge of the roads beyond a 15-mile radius."

Since Henry Ford had refused to chip in to fund Lincoln Highway improvements, and there was growing disinterest among people left off the route, the $10 million fund that Fisher had set up stalled at the halfway point. Joy decided to redirect the association to a new goal: educate the country about the need for good roads made of concrete, with an improved Lincoln Highway as an example. It would be a long journey, however, to reach this goal, as you'll discover throughout this book.

There were also other challenges to address. Between 1915 and 1925, the United States evolved from one named highway (the Lincoln Highway) to an ever-expanding, unorganized, confusing mishmash of named highways, from the Victory Highway to the Dixie Highway. These routes were primarily marked by painted colored bands on telephone poles. Where several named highways shared a route, entire poles would be striped in various colors— confusing indeed. It was time to create an organized, national system of highways, specifically a system of numbered highways.

In 1926, the new United States Numbered Highway System changed the way U.S. drivers navigated the country. Major east–west routes would be numbered in even multiples of 10, while major north–south routes would end in odd numerals. Nearly two-thirds of the Lincoln Highway's length was designated U.S. 30. After this, interest in the Lincoln Highway began to drop considerably.

The LHA ceased activity at the end of 1927. Its last major effort involved marking the highway as a memorial to Abraham Lincoln. On September 1, 1928, thousands of Boy Scouts fanned out along the highway from coast to coast. They installed more than 2,400 concrete markers with a small bust of Lincoln and the inscription, "This highway dedicated to Abraham Lincoln." "They were placed with great hope that this highway would be remembered, even after a system of numbers erased its official status," Hokanson wrote. "The markers are emblems for the Lincoln Highway today. They stand as fragments, like pot shards or ceremonial beads or other objects of a lost culture, a culture overrun by a faster race."

Thanks to efforts like this, stories of Lincoln Highway endured after its official significance was gone. The Lincoln Highway became the backdrop for a weekly half-hour NBC radio show that aired for a few years in the early 1940s on Saturday mornings. The popular radio drama featured the top stars of Broadway and Hollywood, including Ethel Barrymore and Burgess Meredith.

"The Lincoln Highway. Yes, folks, it's the Main Street of America," the broadcaster would proclaim during the program, which was sponsored by Shinola shoe polish and reached 8 million listeners. "Yes, this is the road that links the farms, the mines and the mills of America. And there's nothing that hasn't happened at one time or another along its 3,000 miles."

In the post–World War II era, however, memories of the Lincoln Highway started to fade. The storied highway was growing invisible, especially as new road systems with bypasses, more lanes and ultimately the interstate began to dominate the landscape. Within a relatively short period of time, generations of Americans had never heard of the Lincoln Highway.

Not everyone forgot, however, especially in Iowa. On October 31, 1992, forty-four people from seven states met in a meeting room in Ogden, Iowa, to talk about the future of the Lincoln Highway, preservation of the road and public awareness of the historic highway. They formed the "new" LHA, which led to the creation of state associations in states along the historic highway. Bob Ausberger—a farmer from Jefferson, Iowa, who helped coordinate that initial meeting with his wife, Joyce—served as LHA president from 1994 to 1996.

Since then, interest in the Lincoln Highway, especially in Iowa, has endured. Let's head to Clinton County and begin the journey.

CLINTON COUNTY

When you enter Iowa from the east on the Lincoln Highway, you're in Clinton, which holds the distinction of being the community farthest east in Iowa. Thanks to its prime location near the Mississippi River and the vision of entrepreneurs in the 1800s, Clinton was once known as the lumber capital of the world. Today, you can learn about this fascinating history at the Sawmill Museum.

From the 1850s to the 1890s, there were nearly twenty sawmills operating in Clinton and nearby towns. The Upper Mississippi River offered a practical, easy way to transport logs harvested in the great woods of Minnesota and Wisconsin. The logs would be lashed together to form huge rafts that were guided to sawmills along the river.

Clinton's sawmills provided millions of board feet of lumber that built towns and farms across Iowa, as well as businesses and homes in major cities from Chicago to Kansas City. At one point, Clinton produced one-third of America's lumber, according to the Sawmill Museum.

The decade of the 1880s was one of great expansion in Clinton, when the lumber industry was at its height, according to the *Clinton Herald*. This created a number of multimillionaires in Clinton. These "lumber barons"—including W.J. Young, Chauncey Lamb, David Joyce, the Curtis family and others—built magnificent mansions in Clinton, a few of which remain today. You can visit the exquisite George M. Curtis Mansion at 420 Fifth Avenue South in Clinton. Each room showcases Curtis's lumber products, and every room highlights a different type of wood. A beautiful

When you enter Iowa from the east on the Lincoln Highway, you're in Clinton, which holds the distinction of being the community farthest east in Iowa. Many points in Clinton offer excellent views of the mighty Mississippi River. *Author's collection.*

example of 1880s architecture, this stunning 1883 Queen Anne–style home includes more than forty stained-glass windows, carved banisters, ornate wood trim and massive fireplaces.

The Clinton lumber industry peaked in 1892, with more than 195 million board feet of lumber produced—enough to build about twenty-five thousand houses, businesses and barns, according to the Sawmill Museum. But then came the financial panic of 1893, which cut demand for lumber across the nation. Also, the northern forests were being depleted from decades of intensive logging. The beginning of the end of Clinton's reign in the lumber industry was near, especially as over-logging devastated northern forests.

While Clinton's sawmills are closed and the lumber barons are gone, the city they built is still here. It's also an important community in Iowa's Lincoln Highway heritage. Clinton and the Lincoln Highway made national news in 1919 when the city hosted some noteworthy visitors, including a young lieutenant colonel named Dwight D. Eisenhower, who participated in the first U.S. Army transcontinental motor convoy.

On the afternoon of July 22, 1919, the two-mile-long convoy rolled into the city via the Lincoln Highway. The expedition consisted of eighty-one motorized army vehicles (including trucks, ambulances, motorcycles, a mobile kitchen and more) that were crossing the United States from Washington, D.C., to San Francisco, a venture that covered 3,251 miles in sixty-two days, according to the Eisenhower Presidential Library and Museum. The expedition, which included 24 officers and 258 enlisted men, had been organized following the end of World War I to test the mobility of the military during wartime conditions.

During this arduous trip, Eisenhower learned firsthand how difficult it was to travel great distances on America's roads, which were often impassable and resulted in frequent breakdowns of the military vehicles. These experiences on the Lincoln Highway influenced his decisions as president in the 1950s, when he supported efforts to build America's interstate highway system.

Back in 1919 in Clinton, an estimated fifteen thousand to twenty thousand people attended the festivities, according to news reports. Iowans viewed almost every type of motorized vehicle then in use by the army. Clinton also

By the late 1800s, Clinton was known as the lumber capital of the world. One of the era's lumber barons was George M. Curtis. Every room of the Curtis Mansion in Clinton highlights a different type of wood. *Author's collection.*

hosted a baseball game, band concert and speeches. Clintonians and the troops enjoyed a dance at the Coliseum until the early morning hours.

"The two best crowd pleasers were nocturnal—Jeff the raccoon, who traveled as mascot, and the three-million candle power searchlight," noted the article "Dusty Doughboys on the Lincoln Highway: The 1919 Army Convoy in Iowa," in the May/June 1975 edition of *The Palimpsest*. "Former members of the American Expeditionary Forces interspersed their demonstration of the light with tales from 'over there' about combat between powered aircraft—the first in history."

Tour—and Eat—Your Way through Clinton's History

You can still view some of the historic buildings that members of the 1919 convoy and other early Lincoln Highway travelers saw in Clinton. Visit the website Clinton, Iowa Tourism (www.clintoniowatourism.com) and check out the Historic Walking Tour, where highlights include the Van Allen Building. Built in 1913–15, this National Historic Landmark is a jewel of Clinton's architecture. It was designed by world-famous architect Louis Sullivan, the father of the American skyscraper and mentor of Frank Lloyd Wright.

You can also see the Lafayette Hotel downtown. When it opened in 1906, the Lafayette was said to be the finest hotel in Iowa, complete with marble, mahogany wainscoting and decorative tile and art glass throughout. It provided first-class accommodations for vaudeville stars and other performers who appeared in Clinton, including Lillian Russell, a Clinton native.

To get closer to nature, head up to Eagle Point Park. This beautiful park dates to the late 1800s, when electric-powered trolley cars brought visitors to what was then known as Joyce's Park. During the Great Depression, hundreds of people were hired in Clinton through the Works Progress Administration (WPA) at $15 per week to improve Eagle Point Park, according to the City of Clinton. Roughly $3 million in WPA funds were invested in beautifying Eagle Point Park, which offers panoramic views of the Mississippi River and nearby bluffs.

The famous stone tower (where you can climb inside), limestone footbridge, many trails, "The Lodge" and other amenities were built in the park during this time. Native American artifacts dating to 200 to 600 BC were found in the park during this building period.

Roughly $3 million in WPA funds were invested in the 1930s to beautify Clinton's Eagle Point Park, which includes this famous stone tower and offers panoramic views of the Mississippi River and nearby bluffs. *Courtesy of Digital Grinnell.*

Both the Lincoln Highway and the Archer Daniels Midland (ADM) grain processing plant (shown here with its eye-catching golden dome) have played significant roles in Clinton's economy for decades. *Author's collection.*

This was also a period of lock-and-dam building on the nearby Mississippi River. The Mississippi River has long been used for transportation, but navigation wasn't easy years ago, due to treacherous rapids, submerged rocks and boulders, sandbars, tree snags and water that was sometimes shallow to the point of nonnavigability.

To address these challenges, the U.S. Army Corps of Engineers began creating a "stairway of water" in the 1930s with a series of locks and dams that allow boats and barges to travel safely. Construction of Lock and Dam No. 13 near Clinton began in 1938. Today, thousands of people flock to the Mississippi River each January and February to take part in Bald Eagle Watches. Up to 2,500 bald eagles winter along the Mississippi near the lock and dams.

Before you leave town, don't miss some local culinary specialties. Homer's Deli and Sweetheart Bakery at 241 Main Avenue is a third-generation family-owned business that has served the Clinton area since 1950, as its website notes. The bakery is known for homemade breads, pastries, cakes

The Candlelight Inn, located near the Mississippi River, has been part of Clinton's history since 1967. It's the home of the original "Chicken George," which has been a popular menu item since the 1970s. *Author's collection.*

and its world-famous blarney stones—squares of frosted cake topped with ground salted peanuts. Another local classic is Rastrelli's, which has offered a wide range of enticing Italian and American foods for decades. Then there's the Candlelight Inn near the Mississippi River. Opened in 1967, it's known as the home of the original "Chicken George."

In the early 1970s, founder Bob Prescott was busy serving customers when one of his regulars, Roger Young, came in. Roger asked Bob for "something different." Immediately, Bob thought about his fry cook George's new dish. George was de-boning and cutting up chicken breasts and lightly battering them. He then fried them up and served them—to himself. Bob hadn't tried them yet but asked George to prepare some for Roger, and the rest is history, according to the Candlelight Inn's website.

Roger loved the meal. Soon, people started asking for "Chicken George" before it even made it on the menu. If you search online, you can find a variety of copycat Chicken George recipes, along with "Jan Sauce," which is perfect for dipping. Enjoy!

Chicken George
½ cup ranch dressing
2 teaspoons flour
4 medium boneless chicken breasts
¼ cup each of parmesan cheese and grated cheddar cheese

Preheat oven to 375°F. Mix ranch dressing and flour together. Dredge chicken breasts in mixture. Place in 9-by-13-inch baking dish. Sprinkle grated cheeses on top. Bake for 35 to 45 minutes, until juices run clear and cheese is slightly browned.

Jan Sauce (Copycat)
1 cup mayonnaise
2 tablespoons sugar
2 tablespoons white vinegar
½ teaspoon hot pepper sauce

Mix all ingredients in a small bowl. Let sit for 15 minutes in the refrigerator to allow flavors to blend.

DeWitt Brings the Past Into the Present

As you leave Clinton and head west, you'll arrive in DeWitt, located at the intersection of the Lincoln Highway and the Blues Highway (no. 61). There are plenty of interesting things to see in DeWitt, including the 1878 Opera House and a 1727 German Hausbarn. The barn was originally located in Schleswig-Holstein in northern Germany and was reassembled in DeWitt in 2008 with the help of many community volunteers.

The Hausbarn's exterior retains its historical integrity, including an impressive thatched roof. This unique building is located in DeWitt's Lincoln Park and is home to the DeWitt Chamber and Development Company's office, along with the German Hausbarn Museum.

Around town, you'll find replicas of the artwork of John Bloom (1906–2002), a DeWitt native who embraced the Regionalist style. Bloom participated in Grant Wood's Stone City Art Colony of 1932–33, where he worked alongside Wood, his mentor. *Shucking Corn*, a mural that Bloom

This 1727 German Hausbarn was originally located in Schleswig-Holstein in Germany and was reassembled in DeWitt in 2008. Located in Lincoln Park, it houses the DeWitt Chamber and Development Company and the German Hausbarn Museum. *Author's collection.*

John Bloom (1906–2002), a DeWitt native who studied with master artist and fellow Iowan Grant Wood, painted *Shucking Corn*, in 1937–38. This mural can be found in city hall, which was DeWitt's former post office. *Author's collection.*

painted in 1937–38, can be found at city hall, which was DeWitt's former post office. Bronze statues created from scenes of *Shucking Corn* are located along Sixth Avenue.

Need a place to stay? DeWitt's lodging options include several modern chains, including the AmericInn by the highway interchange on the west edge of town, but some guests in years past preferred the Winsther Motel at 924 Eleventh Street. I felt compelled to stop in and photograph the classic neon sign out front.

The Winsther dates back decades. After Edwin and Esther Soenksen married in 1931 in Lowden (another Iowa Lincoln Highway town just down the road), the couple built and operated the Winsther Motel in DeWitt. Postcards from the 1960s showed a reflecting pool near a decorative lighthouse at the Winsther and listed the motel's hosts as Merle and Betty Smith. Amenities included air conditioning, electric heat, TV, music and phones in every room, along with Tybet's Beauty Salon, which was next door to the office.

When I stopped by the Winsther Motel on a sunny May morning in 2021 to take pictures of the iconic sign out front, owner Joan Keding

The Winsther Motel (shown here in 2011) in DeWitt served travelers for decades. The motel was known for its clean, cozy rooms at an affordable price, as well as its classic neon sign out front. *Author's collection.*

stepped outside to ask if I needed any assistance. I explained what I was up to. "We have a lot of regulars and cater to construction workers," said Kading, who added that guests get clean, cozy rooms at an affordable price, plus free high-speed wireless internet service. The place garners solid reviews online, like "Perfect little hotel. Clean and small, but that's how these old hotels were made. I would gladly stay there again." In June 2022, the *DeWitt Observer* noted that the property was no longer a motel, since a nonprofit group purchased the Winsther for office space and other uses.

As you head west out of DeWitt and Clinton County, you'll soon be surrounded by vast fields of the soybeans and corn that have helped make Iowa a leading agricultural state. This area was once home to a famous Clinton County farmer named Descartes Pascal. Born in 1870, Pascal was a noted photographer and corn cultivator in the Ground Mound area. Some of his exceptional corn was exhibited at a national corn show in Chicago in December 1907, where the corn was named "champion of the world," according to *Wolfe's History of Clinton County* (published in 1911). Farmers continue to raise excellent crops in Iowa, which is the number one corn-producing state in America.

As you head toward Calamus and Wheatland, keep an eye out for new red, white and blue Lincoln Highway markers painted on electrical poles in the area. In the spring of 2022, Calamus-Wheatland Hometown Pride received a grant from Paint Iowa Beautiful and Diamond Vogel (a paint company based in Orange City, Iowa) to paint and restore these highway markers.

CEDAR COUNTY

As you leave Clinton County and enter Cedar County, you'll pass a number of small towns, including Lowden. Although this town was never large, local entrepreneurs saw plenty of potential when the Lincoln Highway came through Cedar County. Cecelia Daehn Clemmens of Lowden was one of those visionaries.

At the time, she was working in the Railroad Hotel in Lowden, which was halfway between Clinton and Cedar Rapids. Well aware that railroad travelers needed food and lodging, she realized that a new kind of traveler of the twentieth century—the automobile tourist—would need the same, according to architectural historian Jan Olive Nash in "The Lincoln Highway in Lowden," which appeared in the spring 1997 edition of *Iowa Heritage Illustrated*.

There was no time to waste. On March 1, 1915, Cecelia Clemmens's husband, Andrew Francis (A.F.) Clemmens, purchased a corner lot near downtown Lowden. Their new hotel, which revealed the influence of Prairie School architecture championed by Frank Lloyd Wright, opened for business on June 17, 1915.

Located at 408 Main Street, the Lincoln Hotel claimed a prime location at the junction of the Hoover Highway (a north–south route named in honor of Herbert Hoover, the only president born in Iowa) and the Lincoln Highway.

The Lincoln Hotel offered rooms for two dollars per night and steak dinners for seventy-five cents. The *Lowden News* pronounced it "one of

Andrew Francis (A.F.) Clemmens and his wife, Cecelia, opened a new hotel in downtown Lowden along the Lincoln Highway in June 1915. Their new hotel revealed the influence of Prairie School architecture. *Courtesy of Lincoln Hotel.*

the finest buildings in the town" and predicted that "situated as it is on the main corner of the Lincoln Highway, it will no doubt receive good patronage."

Emily Post, author of etiquette books and a writer for *Collier's* magazine, rode in one of the estimated five thousand to ten thousand autos that traveled the Lincoln Highway in 1915 to the Panama-Pacific International Exposition in San Francisco. While she didn't stay at the Lincoln Hotel in Lowden, she did comment on what she saw in Iowa and the Midwest: "Every town through the Middle West seems to have a little grill of brick-paved streets; a splendid post office building of stone or brick or marble; a courthouse; and one or two moving picture houses; two or three important-looking dry-goods stores, and some sort of hotel, and in it a lot of drummers [traveling salesmen] in tilted-back chairs exhibiting the soles of their shoes to the street."

Sheltered by a wide porch with Tuscan-style columns, the Lincoln Hotel's front door opened into the lobby, which was near the guests' parlor, dining room and the Clemmenses' living quarters. A dogleg staircase (right-angle staircase) of yellow pine ascended from the lobby to the second-floor central hall, where doors opened into a dozen guest rooms.

Andrew Francis Clemmens and his beloved dog Pal
First owner/proprietor of Lincoln Hotel

Left: Andrew Francis (A.F.) Clemmens shown here on the front porch with his dog, Pal, at his family's Lincoln Hotel, which offered rooms for two dollars per night and steak dinners for seventy-five cents. When the hotel opened in 1915, the *Lowden News* pronounced it "one of the finest buildings in the town." *Courtesy of the Lincoln Hotel.*

Below: The Lincoln Hotel continues to serve travelers in the Lowden area. The hotel offers refurbished suites with private baths, queen-size beds with luxury linens, wireless internet service, spacious seating and a rich history connected to the Lincoln Highway. *Author's collection.*

The hotel thrived in its early years. The Clemmens family managed to keep the Lincoln Hotel going through the Great Depression. After Cecelia was widowed, she sold the business in 1946. While a series of different owners ran the hotel, the building sat vacant for a time, deteriorating slowly from a dozen years of water leaks. In the mid-1990s, it was remodeled extensively and transformed into apartments.

By 1996, the Lincoln Hotel was listed in the National Register of Historic Places. Around this time, the hotel also received the residential Preservation at Its Best Award from the Iowa Historic Preservation Alliance.

In 2001, members of the Model A Ford Club of America and the Iowa Lincoln Highway Association who were driving across Iowa toured the Lincoln Hotel, which had started offering some hotel accommodations that same year. Apartments in the building also remained occupied as the hotel business grew. After the last apartment dwellers moved out in 2004, the hotel has operated solely as a place for travelers ever since.

In March 2017, I was in the area to give a talk about my *Culinary History of Iowa* book at the Clarence Public Library. Before my program that evening, I checked into the Lincoln Hotel, got a quick tour from owner Liz Norton and discovered I was the only guest staying there that evening. (The innkeeper didn't live there, so I'd truly have the place all to myself.) No problem.

As I drifted off to sleep that night at the hotel, I thought about all the guests who had stayed here long before me. My spacious guest room would have encompassed three or four small hotel rooms decades ago. The bathroom would have been at the end of the hall, shared by everyone, since individual rooms didn't have their own private baths. Had it been a hot summer day, guests in those days before air conditioning and television likely wouldn't have spent much time in their room anyway. They would have gathered on the front porch to visit and enjoy a cool breeze.

When I checked out the next morning, I hoped the Lincoln Hotel would carry on its unique legacy. I'm pleased to report it's doing fine, thanks to Don and Mary Schliff, Melissa and Jim Hardman and Robert and Tanya Schliff, all from California.

Don and Mary bought the hotel in November 2017 from Liz and Brad Norton. "Don and I stayed at the Lincoln Hotel while visiting family and friends in the Wheatland area," said Mary, who grew up in Wheatland, a Lincoln Highway town east of Lowden. "Our children and their families often joined us there. We loved the hotel, the wonderful hospitality and the small-town atmosphere—a great break from Los Angeles."

During a summer visit in 2017, the Schliff family noticed a "For Sale" sign outside the Lincoln Hotel. "We were heartbroken because we couldn't imagine not staying at this wonderful old hotel when we came to Iowa," Mary said. "We were more concerned that it might be turned into apartments or eventually torn down, as has happened to so many historic buildings in small towns."

History is important to Mary and her family, who own a farm east of Wheatland along the original Lincoln Highway. (Their family has owned this farmland since 1908, making it a Century Farm, a designation given to land that's been owned by the same family for at least one hundred years.) As they weighed their options, the family decided to buy the hotel.

Today, the Lincoln Hotel offers four suites, which were refurbished in 2019. All the rooms have private baths, queen-size beds with luxury linens, wireless internet service and spacious seating. "We appreciate the Lincoln Hotel for its unique architecture, its place in American transportation history and its connection to the Lincoln Highway and Lowden," Mary said.

Lincoln Highway Shootout Included Local Vigilantes

Not all Lincoln Highway travelers in Cedar County have come through looking for a place to stay. When the Great Depression intensified in the early 1930s, it unleashed one of the most prolific periods in American history for daring bank robberies. Even the tiny town of Stanwood along the Lincoln Highway became a target.

The *Lisbon News* reported that a robbery occurred around noon on February 2, 1932, at the Union Trust and Savings Bank in Stanwood. R.D. Forbes (who occasionally used the alias "Robert Morse"), thirty-five, and Robert Wall, twenty-nine, forced Otto Evers, the bank's vice-president, and C.H. Haesemeyer, a cashier, into the bank vault. The criminals also ordered customer Walter Lehrman into the vault.

The criminals stole about $500 during the heist. (That would be worth more than $10,000 in 2022 dollars.) The burglars escaped in a Model T Ford headed west on the Lincoln Highway. At the first T-intersection outside Stanwood, they transferred to a Model A Ford they'd parked there before the crime and then headed back east. As the criminals approached Lowden, a group of five local vigilantes—including M.V. "Walt" Pauls, Lowden's town

Lincoln Highway scene of shootout

Happy birthday, Lincoln Highway. Our nation's first transcontinental automobile route turns 100 this year — officially on Oct. 31, 1913.

But, the Lincoln Highway has always been a favorite Ramblin' topic, whether it's the Youngville Cafe or the Tama bridge or old routes in Cedar County or through Marion and Cedar Rapids. So, what better way to wind down my Gazette career than write about it in this, my second to last column? (My final Ramblin' column runs Wednesday.)

A lot is going on this year with the biggie being the Lincoln Highway Association's (lincolnhighwayassoc.org) 100th Anniversary Tour along the original route, gravel roads and all. Cars leave Times Square in New York City on June 21 and San Francisco on June 22 to

Bonnie May Pauls scrapbook photo

These five men formed a vigilante group in 1932 to stop bank robbers who had escaped from Stanwood and drove toward Lowden along the Lincoln Highway. From left are an unidentified man, Hans Andreson, A.F. Clemmens, Roy Marks and Lowden Town Marshal M.V. Pauls. The photo appeared in the Feb. 3, 1932, Cedar Rapids Evening Gazette and Republican.

converge in Kearney, Neb., on June 30 for the centennial celebration and conference.

The Lincoln Highway ties in with a follow-up to my Feb. 25 column when I asked readers about five vigilantes posing with guns in front of a Ford Model A in a photo sent by Keith Techau of Lis-

bon. The picture was in a scrapbook owned by Bonnie Pauls of Mechanicsville who died Aug. 9, 2010, at age 96.

Several folks responded, but Keith nailed it when he ran across a Lisbon News story about the robbery of the Union Trust and Savings Bank in Stanwood on Feb. 2, 1932. It

says one bandit, R.D. Forbes, 35, was killed and the other, Robert Wall, 29, captured in Lowden after the noon robbery that netted $500. They escaped in a Model-T, driving west on the Lincoln Highway.

Outside of Stanwood, they transferred to a Model A and turned around. As they came to Lowden, a group of vigilantes — M. V. Pauls (Town Marshal), A.F. Clemmens, Hans Andreson and Roy Marks — had blocked the road. The shootout ensued. Forbes was shot in the back seat of the car.

Pauls, Bonnie's father-in-law, was identified far right in the photo by several people, including Marilyn Benishek of Belle Plaine who is his niece. "Walt got shot in the leg," she said. "He didn't get hurt too bad but he limped the rest of his life." He died in 1970.

The robbers were identified after Wall told authorities to check at 1011 Second Ave. SE in Cedar Rapids. So, I checked out The Gazette.

On Feb. 3, this newspaper ran the photo, identifying the four men on the right standing in front of the bandits' stolen car. The story's details said Forbes had lived in Stanwood, where his father was a barber, until age 10. As a contract painter, Wall had done work at the Cedar Rapids Police Department in 1931.

By then, the Lincoln Highway through Iowa was Highway 30. But, as "The Main Street Across America" with 2,400 Boy Scouts markers placed along the road and icons such as the late George Preston's sign-decorated service station in Belle Plaine, fans have kept it alive for a century.

● Comments: (319) 398-8323; dave.rasdal@sourcemedia.net

On February 2, 1932, two men robbed the Union Trust and Savings Bank in Stanwood, stole about $500 and tried to escape via the Lincoln Highway. Local law enforcement officers and vigilantes soon caught them. Years later, a columnist at the *Gazette* in Cedar Rapids recapped those dramatic events. *Courtesy of Lincoln Highway Museum.*

marshal; A.F. Clemmens of the Lincoln Hotel; Hans Andreson; Roy Marks; and Lawrence Kemmann—blocked the road.

A shootout commenced. Forbes died at the scene, and authorities captured Walls. A photo of the five vigilantes gathered around the burglars' getaway car (with a bullet-shattered window clearly visible) appeared in the February 3, 1932 edition of the *Cedar Rapids Evening Gazette and Republican* newspaper. The article noted that Forbes had lived in Stanwood until age ten, and his father was the barber in Stanwood.

In 2013, Dave Rasdal of the *Cedar Rapids Gazette* wrote a column titled "Lincoln Highway Scene of Shootout" recalling this dramatic incident. He quoted Marilyn Benishek of Belle Plaine, who noted that Pauls had been shot in the leg and "didn't get hurt too bad, but he limped the rest of his life" before he died in 1970.

TOWN MARSHAL'S DAUGHTER DESCRIBED "LIGHTNING-FAST" EVENTS

Vanita Pauls Fisher, Walt Pauls's daughter, shared more details of that remarkable day. The Lowden Historical Society included her story from 1976 on the IowaGenWeb.org website. She was a senior in high school in 1932 and recalled coming home from school to eat lunch on February 2: "Upon arriving home, my father, M.V. Pauls, who was the town marshal and also a local member of a vigilance committee, was informed by another vigilante that the group was being summoned—the bank in Stanwood had just been robbed. Father left with the vigilantes. After eating dinner, I went back to school for the afternoon classes. My arrival at school turned into a state of alarm."

Students whispered to one another as Vanita approached. "I was aware that something must have happened to Dad. I soon learned the shocking news that he had been shot by one of the bandits, but I was later relieved when assured that it was only a wound in the right leg."

The Lowden vigilantes raced west out of town on the Lincoln Highway in August Malottki's pickup truck. Ray Marks worked for Malottki, who owned the local meat market, Fisher noted. About a mile west of Lowden, the vigilantes spotted a late-model Model A Ford approaching Lowden from the west. Since people had seen the bank robbers fleeing west in a Model T, the vigilantes stopped the Model A to ask if they'd seen the getaway car.

"As my father approached the stopped car, a man in the back seat opened fire," Fisher said. "A newspaper article explained, 'A.F. Clemmens fired a riot gun through the window of the bandits' car and wounded one bandit.'"

The man in the rear seat jumped out and ran to the back of the vehicle for protection. Marshal Pauls shot and killed him, although the hail of bullets damaged Pauls's leg. As one bandit lay dead on the highway, the other thief was still seated behind the getaway car's steering wheel. He raised his hands and surrendered. "Had the outlaws not been so hasty in opening fire, they may have eluded their captors," noted Fisher's account of the shootout.

CARS WERE FULL OF WEAPONS

When the coroner inspected the dead man's body, he found $575 in bills inside Forbes's shirt and six $1 bills in his trouser pocket. The clothing Forbes was wearing when he died was not the same garb he wore during the holdup.

People later found a black overcoat and shirt near the high bridge over the railroad track west of Lowden, Fisher said.

Vanita continued, "The man was undoubtedly in the act of changing clothes when the car was stopped by the officers. He wore a pair of Oxfords that were untied at the time of his death, and the bankers remembered the man as wearing high-top shoes."

Authorities also searched the Model T, which the robbers used in the first part of the escape. The car, which had Benton County, Iowa license plates, contained several pistols, a shotgun, sledgehammers and bars. The Model A Ford, which was registered in the name of Robert Morse, had New Mexico plates. It was equipped with a radio and gun holster on the steering column. The back seat contained a Texas Ranger rifle, two chisels, a small maul, four or five new flat-iron handles and several suitcases full of clothing.

Wall was convicted for his role in the bank robbery, noted the April 12, 1932 edition of the *Davenport Daily Times* newspaper. Judge Atherton B. Clark of Tipton sentenced Wall to the state penitentiary in Fort Madison, Iowa, according to the article "Stanwood Bank Robber Gets 25 Years in Prison."

ROCK ON IN CLARENCE

Down the road from Lowden and Stanwood, take time to check out the quirky, fun attractions in Clarence, one of the Iowa communities where the Lincoln Highway still passes through the downtown area. Notice the four Lincoln Highway logo crosswalks. Volunteers worked together on May 27, 2022, to paint the crosswalks, a project supported, in part, by a grant from Paint Iowa Beautiful, Keep Iowa Beautiful and Diamond Vogel.

While you're in Clarence, check out the larger-than-life library book outside the Clarence Public Library. If you like modern farmhouse décor

This colorful mural in downtown Clarence honors the town's Lincoln Highway heritage, as well as other local history. The community was originally called Onion Grove because of the wild onions that grew nearby. *Author's collection.*

and vintage treasures, stop by Onion Grove Mercantile (a nod to the town's original name of Onion Grove), which also includes a hand-painted sign-design studio.

You might spot Elvis in a pink-and-white classic Ambassador car outside a home along Highway 30. It's a prelude to the prime photo opportunities at the Hound Dog Rock Shop, which is housed in a former Lincoln Highway gas station. Owners Kirk and Janel Wenndt sell an impressive array of rocks, minerals, gems, geodes, crystals and custom-made jewelry from local, national and international locations. Rock on!

LINN COUNTY

Once you cruise through Mechanicsville and leave Cedar County, you've entered Linn County. Imagine, for a moment, you're making the trip in a vintage Ford Model T.

On June 4, 1924, the ten millionth Ford Model T rolled off the assembly line in Michigan. Henry Ford posed for publicity photos as he stood between this Model T and his 1896 Quadricycle—the first car he made.

Ford and his team had introduced the Model T to the world in 1908. Ford wanted the Model T to be affordable, simple to operate and durable. As it was one of the first mass-produced vehicles, the Ford Motor Company could sell the car for $850 (the equivalent of roughly $26,000 in 2022 dollars), with the price dropping as low as $290 by 1926.

In 1924, Ford sent the ten millionth Model T on a cross-country tour along the Lincoln Highway from New York to California to promote his company. The July 12, 1924 edition of the *Moline Dispatch* newspaper ran the Associated Press story "Ten Millionth Ford Crosses Iowa on Transcontinental Tour." The article noted that driver Frank Kulick, the famed auto racer, had driven one of Henry Ford's first cars across the continent in 1903. "That first trip was a 23-day sentence at hard labor," said Kulick, recalling how there were no marked highways back then. "Now, Kulick's way is plainly set out to him by markers at every corner," the article continued. "Every condition of the road is known in advance, and the driver is warned of dangerous curves and railroad crossings by signs nearly as numerous as frightened horses in the old days."

In 1924, Henry Ford sent the ten millionth Model T on a Lincoln Highway tour from New York to California. The car returned to Iowa when it made another coast-to-coast trip in June 1974 along the Lincoln Highway. Everywhere it stopped, including Mount Vernon, it attracted plenty of interested onlookers. *Courtesy of Mount Vernon Historic Preservation Commission.*

The ten millionth Model T eventually returned to Iowa when Dr. Alan Hathaway, a dentist in Davenport, purchased the car. Hathaway (who died in 2016 at age eighty-six) honored the fiftieth anniversary of the ten millionth Model T's cross-country journey by driving his own coast-to-coast trip in early June 1974 along the Lincoln Highway. Everywhere he stopped in Iowa, from Mount Vernon to Ames and beyond, the Model T attracted plenty of onlookers and media coverage.

By the time Hathaway made his journey, paved roads had been the norm for generations. Things were much different, however, in the early years of the Lincoln Highway. By 1922, Iowa had only 334 miles of paved road, representing only 5 percent of the total road milage, according to Drake Hokanson, author of *The Lincoln Highway: Main Street Across America.* Iowa turned into a 300-mile-long mudhole when it rained.

So why wasn't Iowa improving its roads? Blame an unequal property tax structure that placed a greater burden on farmers when it came to funding road improvement. This created "a general dislike for the notion of expensive, high-type roads," noted the Lincoln Highway Association's

(LHA) "Object Lesson: The Seedling Mile in Linn County, Iowa," a booklet published in 2004. The irony was that Iowans were spending enough in (road) maintenance to have amortized the cost of hard-surfaced construction in a few years, the booklet added. "Even LHA President Henry Joy said they [Iowans] were practically rebuilding their dirt roads every summer and having them washed out by storms or torn up by struggling traffic every winter."

Joy lambasted Iowa for its poor roads: "Today, in the rich state of Iowa, not a wheel turns outside the paved streets of her cities during or for some time after the frequent, heavy rains. Every farm is isolated. School attendance is impossible. Transportation is at a standstill. Millions of dollars of wheeled vehicles become, for the time being, worthless."

While LHA backers originally tried to raise $10 million for improvements to the highway across America, that idea was eventually scaled back to paving "seedling miles" of concrete. The seedling mile program encouraged communities in rural states like Iowa to pave mile-long sections of the Lincoln Highway. It was hoped that these stretches of concrete would spur interest in additional road improvements.

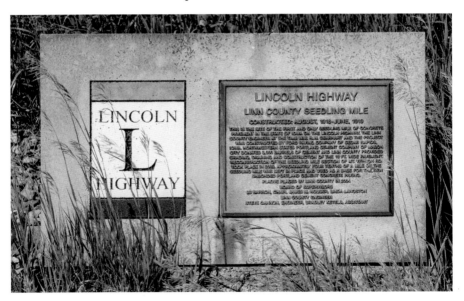

While Lincoln Highway Association backers originally tried to raise $10 million to improve the highway across America, that idea was scaled back to paving "seedling miles" of concrete. The seedling mile program encouraged communities in rural states like Iowa to pave mile-long sections of the highway to show the benefits of improved roads. *Author's collection.*

The LHA required that seedling miles be located in rural areas, at least six miles from any town, at places where the topography made travel difficult. "The idea was that once a driver was on the paved mile and could speed along unfettered and then suddenly dropped back onto an unpaved, often mud, road, the drama of this contrast would demonstrate better than any other means the wisdom of paved roads," according to the LHA's 2004 booklet.

The first seedling mile was built in 1914 near Malta, Illinois. When LHA representatives proposed a seedling mile in Iowa, they had eight thousand barrels of donated cement available. Four counties expressed interest, including Linn, Greene, Marshall and Pottawattamie.

Linn County had some heavy hitters, including Willis Haskell, a state senator from Cedar Rapids, and Edward Killian, a well-known businessman from Cedar Rapids. Killian owned Killian's department store, which touted itself as the largest department store in Iowa on the Lincoln Highway, complete with a tea room, post office services and public restrooms.

These influential men's seedling mile proposal to the Linn County Board of Supervisors worked. Construction on the seedling mile began in Linn County in August 1918, with cement donated by the Northwestern States Portland Cement Company in Mason City through the LHA. The Ford Paving Company of Cedar Rapids managed the project.

The seedling mile was located about halfway between Cedar Rapids, Marion and Mount Vernon, on what historically had been an old wagon road and stagecoach trail, according to the LHA's 2004 booklet. The location also had political implications for Cedar Rapids and Marion, with both communities fighting for the county seat designation and access to the Lincoln Highway.

While the seedling mile was slated for completion on November 1, 1918, the job wasn't done until June 1919. Even though the contractor had modern equipment like steam shovels, he had trouble finding enough labor. (This was the era of the Spanish influenza pandemic and World War I.) Ten straight days of rain didn't help anything either.

Jean (Stoneking) Moore recalled how the workers paving the road lived in a tent camp across the road from her father's house. Her grandmother cooked meals for the workers, many of whom were Russian and Irish immigrants.

No seedling miles were constructed after 1919. The LHA felt that the seedling mile program had proven the value of paved roads, so the group shifted its focus to developing standards for modern road construction.

Linn County boasted the first seedling mile in Iowa along the Lincoln Highway. This paved mile of the highway was located about halfway between Cedar Rapids, Marion and Mount Vernon. Today, signage denotes the significance of this historic section of the road, which was paved in 1918–19. *Author's collection.*

Not only could motorists get their car repaired back in the day at Stearn's Garage in Mount Vernon, but Lincoln Highway travelers could also get a quick sense of distances from Mount Vernon to various cities, just by glancing at the building. *Courtesy of Mount Vernon Historic Preservation Commission.*

While motorists liked driving on the seedling mile in Linn County, road improvement in Iowa didn't get the big boost it needed until 1921. The passage of the Federal Highway Act that year provided millions of matching funds to the states for highway construction. By 1928, the entire length of the Lincoln Highway across Iowa was either graveled or paved. The June 16, 1930 edition of the *Des Moines Register* proclaimed that "Iowa has stepped out of the mud!"

By 1931, paving of the Lincoln Highway from New York to Missouri Valley, Iowa, was complete, as noted in the LHA's "Object Lesson." Within the next few years, the remaining portions connecting to Council Bluffs would also be reconstructed, completing the paving of Iowa's portion of the Lincoln Highway.

Mount Vernon Barn Showcases *American Gothic*

When you're in Linn County near Mount Vernon, make time to explore this charming small town. Not only is it the home of Cornell College, but it also hosts the annual, open-air Lincoln Highway Nitty Gritty (formerly known as the Fourth of July Antiques Extravaganza), with vendors from across the country. In 2022, the community also came together for the twelfth annual Mount Vernon Chocolate Stroll in June to celebrate all things chocolate. If neither event is going on when you stop by, check out the Lincoln Wine Bar and enjoy wood-fired pizza in a relaxed setting.

As you travel west of Mount Vernon on the paved, four-lane Highway 30, you might be surprised to see a rendition of Grant Wood's famous *American Gothic* painted on a barn. "It definitely stands out from a landscape," said Mark Benesh, a Mount Vernon middle school art teacher who painted the barn.

It started around 2007, when the barn's owner connected with Benesh during Chalk the Walk, an event where more than two hundred artists use Mount Vernon's Main Street as a canvas to create stunning works of chalk art. "She asked me if I knew anyone who painted barn murals, but I didn't," Benesh said.

Undeterred, the barn owner asked him again next year. He decided that he could give it a try. First, the barn had to be faced with cement board. "This material doesn't expand and contract with the weather like barn wood does, which helps the paint last longer," Benesh explained.

After the barn owner paid for the rights to reproduce the *American Gothic* image, Benesh created a grid system to scale, based on a photo he took of the

While this barn west of Mount Vernon is located along four-lane Highway 30, it's not far from the Lincoln Highway. "It definitely stands out from the landscape," said Mark Benesh, a Mount Vernon middle school art teacher who painted a rendition of Grant Wood's famous *American Gothic* on the barn in 2008. *Author's collection.*

barn. "It's the kind of deal where 1 inch equals one foot on the grid," said Benesh, who noted that the barn measures about thirty by forty feet. "Then you just paint square by square."

It took Benesh about three weeks to complete the barn-sized *American Gothic*. He used artist-quality acrylic paint and a varnish to help protect the image from ultraviolet light. "I haven't had to touch it up since I painted it in 2008," said Benesh, who also painted flowers and deer on the east side of the barn, along with buffalo on the west side.

Travelers often stop to photograph the colorful barn. "Rural Iowa's landscape is so interesting with all its patterns and colors," said Benesh, a Mount Vernon native. "Anything can be beautiful if you handle it properly."

This is something that native Iowan Grant Wood (1891–1942) knew well. Born on a farm near Anamosa, Wood became a prominent member of the Regionalist art movement. Wood spent much of his life in Cedar Rapids, including 5 Turner Alley, where he lived and worked from 1924 to 1935. This light-filled loft, where he painted *American Gothic* in 1930, is open for public tours. You can also view a number of Wood's paintings at the Cedar Rapids Museum of Art.

Gangsters Dined at the Lighthouse Inn

When you're in the Cedar Rapids area, don't miss the Lighthouse Inn at 6905 Mount Vernon Road Southeast. This is as classic a piece of Lincoln Highway history as you'll find anywhere in Iowa.

Built in 1912, the Lighthouse Inn was originally a small joint where locals and travelers could enjoy drinks and dinner and maybe rent one of the cabins that used to sit behind the restaurant. (Guests could avoid the higher hotel tax charged within Cedar Rapids' city limits.)

When it opened, the Lighthouse Inn was out in the country, on a rutted farm-to-market road. Although the supper club was built far from a lake or ocean, two small stone lighthouses graced the front entrance of this Lincoln Highway hotspot. (The lighthouses were destroyed years ago, however, when a truck driver fell asleep at the wheel and crashed into them.)

With its rural location, the Lighthouse Inn didn't have the law looking over its shoulder the way city restaurants did during Prohibition. It became one of the spots where a savvy traveler could still obtain an illegal drink of alcohol. In that era, it became a popular stop for Chicago-area mobsters looking to beat the heat until things cooled off in the Windy City.

The Lighthouse Inn at 6905 Mount Vernon Road Southeast, Cedar Rapids, is as classic a piece of Lincoln Highway history as you'll find anywhere in Iowa. Built in 1912, the Lighthouse Inn has attracted guests of all kinds (including gangsters in the 1930s) and maintains its old-school, supper club style. *Author's collection.*

"Yes, Al Capone dined here, as did John Dillinger," notes the Lighthouse Inn's website and its menus. "If you're sitting in the booth to the left of the lounge entrance, that's exactly where Dillinger's gun went off and left a hole in the wall. Even though it is no longer there, it is still a part of our history."

By some accounts, Capone chose to frequent the Lighthouse Inn because the Lincoln Highway was the only hard-surfaced road in the area at that time. Capone refused to take a chance on Iowa's dirt and gravel roads, for fear of getting stuck if rain turned the roads to mud.

While the 1930s-era mobsters are gone, the Lighthouse Inn maintains a nautical theme and a calm, relaxed feel reminiscent of a midwestern supper club. When I met some of my family members there for dinner in December 2020, I savored the exceptional history of this place, along with the delectable steak. Whether you like prime rib, shrimp, barbecued ribs or other classics, don't miss an opportunity to dine at one of the oldest continuously operating restaurants in Iowa.

Remembering the Rosdail Café and Service Truck Stop

Just as Linn County's seedling mile helped spur the development of improved roads, better roads helped America's trucking industry grow in the 1930s. As the number of trucking companies increased, entrepreneurs like the Rosdail family of Cedar Rapids benefited.

By the 1940s, they were running the Rosdail Café and Service Truck Stop on the northwest side of Cedar Rapids, three blocks west of the junction of Highway 30 and 149. Their business card promoted "cigarettes, showers, free bunks for truckers, home cooking, 100% union, and 24-hour service, phone 3-0486."

Ike Rosdail operated the business, along with his daughters Hope and Joyce. While they ran a café with a few gas pumps outside for motorists, the truck stop was big business here. It was especially noteworthy because of the truck dispatcher, according to the article "Don't Talk Back to Hope Rosdail: In Fact, She Tells Them Where to Head In," in the Sunday, June 28, 1942 edition of the *Cedar Rapids Gazette*.

"Keeping track of 48 men at one time is a feat, no matter how you view it, but Miss Hope Rosdail of Cedar Rapids keeps track of exactly that many, in spite of the fact that they're scattered along the highways between Chicago

Left: As the number of trucking companies increased by the early 1940s, entrepreneurs like the Rosdail family of Cedar Rapids benefited. They ran the Rosdail Café and Service Truck Stop on the northwest side of Cedar Rapids, shown here with Hope Rosdail and her sister, Joyce. *Courtesy of Roz Schultes.*

Below: Truck dispatcher Hope Rosdail of Cedar Rapids welcomed this new "Victory" truck that pulled into the Rosdail Café and Service Truck Stop on its way east in 1942. Painted red, white and blue, with slogans like "For Victory Buy Stamps and Bonds," the truck helped promote the war effort. *Courtesy of Roz Schultes.*

and Denver," reported the article. "At 24, Miss Rosdail is probably the only woman truck dispatcher in the country."

While Rosdail described her job as "settling all their little griefs," writer Dora Jane Hamblin noted that the complex job involved checking in trucks, assigning drivers, settling legal difficulties like fines and summons for overloading, handing out paychecks, arranging vacations and "picking up drivers in the city who are arranging to take the trucks on."

"Anything can happen, and almost everything did when I first took over the job, but it gets to be pretty much routine after awhile," Rosdail said.

At the time, Cedar Rapids was a relay point on the Chicago-Denver truck line, where new drivers were assigned to take trucks west to Blair, Nebraska, and east to Chicago. As a dispatcher, Rosdail ensured that loads went through promptly and trucks were in good traveling condition, reported the newspaper.

By 1942, trucks were coming in at all hours of the day and night. In June 1942, the company's new "Victory" truck pulled into the Rosdail's service station on its way east. Painted red, white and blue, with slogans like "For Victory Buy Stamps and Bonds," the truck was the first of five of its kind to promote the war effort. "The boys fixed it up because our company is now working on a government contract, and all the drivers are buying bonds and stamps," Hope Rosdail told the newspaper.

Before trucks accounted for a larger percentage of the traffic on the Lincoln Highway, this route had been a key connector for bootleggers, gangsters and other assorted characters during Prohibition. Living near the Lincoln Highway remained an adventure when Ike Rosdail's granddaughter Roz (Rosdail) Schultes was growing up in Cedar Rapids in the 1950s and 1960s. Her father, Merle "Bud" Rosdail, and his family lived near the area that would later include the Cedar Hills housing development. "I remember Grandpa and Dad talking about the bootleggers and Chicago gangsters who used to come through this area," Schultes said.

Schultes's parents bought their home at 228 Harnett Street Northwest from John Cox, a well-known bootlegger. "This was a rural area outside Cedar Rapids' city limits back then," said Schultes, who remembers gravel roads in the neighborhood. "John Cox made corn whiskey and would bury the hooch in the cornfield behind the fence line by our house."

If family lore didn't convince you that bootleggers and gangsters worked this area years ago, the spooky tunnel below Grandpa Ike's gas station on Johnson Avenue would make you a believer. "I saw the steps going down to a tunnel system," said Schultes, who recalled her father and grandfather telling stories about bootleggers and Chicago gangsters who'd hide out down there. "When I was a kid, we'd go down there into the pitch black, but we'd get scared and come back out. The old timers said those tunnels extended a few miles to downtown Cedar Rapids and the Cedar River."

While the Rosdails weren't involved in any illegal activities, they knew that some "extracurricular activities" occurred in their midst during those turbulent days of the 1930s. Supper clubs around the area were often a favorite gathering place not only for regular customers and travelers but also for shadier characters. "You had all these supper clubs, from the Lighthouse Inn in Cedar Rapids on the Lincoln Highway to the Ranch Supper Club down towards Swisher and Iowa City, and all those places had their back rooms," Schultes said.

For those not involved in bootlegging and other illegal activities, there was a "live and let live" attitude. "Everyone knew about those back-room deals, but they just looked the other way and hoped the place didn't get raided when they were eating there or working there," Schultes said.

Stories of bootlegging and Chicago mobsters would follow Schultes when she married her husband, Rick, in 1984 and moved to his family's farm southeast of Templeton in western Iowa, south of the Lincoln Highway. "When my dad found out Rick was from Templeton, he said, 'Oh yeah, we know all about Templeton rye over here,'" hinting at the legendary Iowa whiskey's ties to infamous customers like Al Capone.

THE CED-REL:
FROM KEY CLUB/SPEAKEASY TO SUPPER CLUB

Schultes has many fond memories of life along the Lincoln Highway, including the Ced-Rel Supper Club, just west of Cedar Rapids. "When you had any special occasion, you wanted to go to the Ced-Rel, which was known for its steaks and seafood, including lobster," said Schultes, who enjoyed a drink there on her twenty-first birthday. "That place was busy all the time."

This legendary supper club at 11909 Sixteenth Avenue Southwest/ Highway 30 West got its start around 1926 (as best as anyone can remember) as a gas station and café called Whip's, named after the owner, Whip Luenzi. In 1935, Verlin "Stretch" Sedrel and his wife, Isabelle, purchased the property and held a contest to rebrand it. The winning name was a play on the couple's last name, and an eastern Iowa destination was born. For many of the years the Sedrels owned it, the restaurant operated like a members-

The legendary Ced-Rel west of Cedar Rapids opened around 1926 and evolved into
a members-only key club (and destination for all manner of nefarious activities, from
drinking to gambling). It later became a family-friendly supper club that served the area for
generations, although it shut down after the August 2020 derecho. *Author's collection.*

only key club and served steaks, seafood and appetizers, including the Ced-Rel's homemade bean pot, a savory dish of baked pinto beans.

People didn't just go to the Ced-Rel for the food though. "During that time, it was a destination for all manner of nefarious activities, from drinking to gambling," wrote Megan Bannister in her book *Iowa Supper Clubs*. "The restaurant doubled as a speakeasy that allowed its key-holding members to imbibe without worry."

Traces of this history remained decades later. "The original door is still there where they could see out, but nobody could see in," former owner Pat Snyder told the *Cedar Rapids Gazette* in February 1994. "If members forgot their keys, a doorman could identify them through the window on his side and admit them. Otherwise, the one-way window kept the club private."

On March 20, 1948, the Linn County sheriff, deputies and two Cedar Rapids detectives raided the Ced-Rel. The sheriff seized sixty-three bottles of liquor from the premises, as well as seven slot machines, which local newspapers called "one-armed bandits."

The Sedrels and their manager, Joe King, were charged with illegal possession and sale of liquor and illegal possession of gambling devices. According to a May 12, 1948 article from the *Gazette*, the group was fined a total of $1,300 (that's about $15,300 in 2022 dollars). The money from the slot machines was ordered to be given to the local school fund. The liquor—with the exception of four bottles that were returned because they had been taken from the upper floor and deemed not part of the restaurant stock—was offered to local hospitals for medicinal purposes, Bannister noted. (In case you're wondering why all this was happening after national Prohibition ended in December 1933, Iowa became one of the original "control" or "monopoly" states in 1934. The state assumed direct control over the wholesale and retail distribution of all alcoholic beverages, except beer. Not until 1963 was the Class C liquor license created, allowing the sale of alcoholic beverages by the drink for on-premises consumption.)

Given the potential consequences of another citation, the Sedrels decided to open their private club to the public. In 1949, the Sedrels also added a private party room in the supper club to accommodate larger groups and special events.

After the Sedrels sold the supper club in 1958 to Bob Snyder and his wife, Pat, the Snyders added a distinctive tropical theme to the party room, which they called the "Bamboo Room." The people who were part of the Ced-Rel during this era helped make the place unforgettable. Consider Luanna "Lu" Happel, who was seventy-two when Dave Rasdal wrote the

2012 *Gazette* story "Temporary Help Leads to 50 Years and Counting as Bartender at Ced-Rel."

"Luanna Happel only meant to help out friends Bob and Pat Snyder at their Ced-Rel Supper Club during the holiday season. It was 1962, the restaurant along Highway 30 west of Cedar Rapids was always hopping and there was a shortage of workers. 'I said, 'I'll just come out and help you for Christmas,' Lu laughs. 'I never left.'"

In that era before liquor by the drink was legal, customers who wanted a cocktail had to bring their own liquor bottle into restaurants. Then they'd order a setup, consisting of ice and a mixer like Coca-Cola or ginger ale to pour into their whiskey, bourbon or other liquor of choice. Happel sold setups at the bar for a quarter. Customers gathered around the Ced-Rel's bar to drink, play cards and smoke.

Happel stuck with the Ced-Rel after the Snyders sold the supper club to Ken and Mary Selzer in 2002, and their son, Jeff Selzer, assumed ownership in 2010. Happel spent fifty-four years at the Ced-Rel before she passed away in 2016. No matter how lively the crowd might get, there was nothing Happel couldn't handle. In 2012, Jeff Selzer told the *Gazette* that Happel was known to slam her hand down on the bar if folks got a little too rowdy. "This is my bar," Happel said. "We don't talk about politics. We don't talk about religion. We talk about sex," which always brought plenty of laughs. Everything was fine. "There's only one Lu," Jeff added.

Through the years, the Ced-Rel won local awards like the KCRG TV 9 A-List Award for best steakhouse. Customers also loved the broasted chicken, ribs and Iowa pork loin. Each entrée came with a classic relish tray (with an assortment of carrots; radishes; pickles; crackers with homemade cottage cheese dip; deep-fried chicken livers; homemade, tangy meatballs; and fresh-battered, crispy onion rings). If that weren't enough, the meal included a crisp, tossed lettuce salad and choice of potato, baked beans or dinner rolls.

While the Ced-Rel was a sit-down restaurant, complete with spacious tables and comfortable, cushioned red vinyl booths, it almost became a drive-thru one afternoon in 1985. Dan Degner, twenty-three, of Dysart, Iowa, was heading east on the highway but lost control of his semitruck as he tried to slow down for another vehicle. His truck, loaded with fifty thousand pounds of soybeans, plowed into the dining room (which was empty at the time, thank goodness). The building's main support beam prevented the truck from barreling all the way through the restaurant.

The accident made front-page news, complete with some shocking photos of the truck in the dining room. The December 20, 1985 edition of the

Gazette noted that the Ced-Rel's dining room was only thirty-three feet from the highway. "All I could think of was, 'I hope to hell nobody's in there eating,'" said Degner, who escaped unscathed, other than a few cuts on one hand and a sore neck.

When I ate in the dining room in early June 2018, the Ced-Rel conveyed a timeless quality that made you feel like you were stepping back into the past. I visited with April Urell, who became the Ced-Rel's new owner in 2014 after having worked as a server there since 2003. After enjoying a fantastic steak dinner, I vowed I'd be back again. But then came 2020 with the COVID-19 pandemic and the devastating derecho (an inland hurricane) that tore through the area on August 10, 2020. It was too much for the Ced-Rel, which has been closed for months now. But if you'd like a virtual taste of this classic supper club, you can still visit the Ced-Rel's website at https://ced-rel.com.

BENTON COUNTY

As you head into Benton County along Highway 30, you might spot a pink barn on the north side of the highway. Why is that barn pink? Well, it has been that way ever since Hope (Rosdail) Kolsto was involved. (Yes, the same Hope who was the truck dispatcher in Linn County in the 1940s.)

After Hope married Kenneth Kolsto, the couple farmed near Atkins. Hope also began baking elaborate wedding cakes for local brides. When they would tell her how hard it was to find the right wedding gown, she decided to renovate the barn (complete with plenty of shag carpeting) to create Hope's Bridal Boutique in 1973. Back then, the shop had more than one hundred different wedding gowns in stock (ranging from $100 to $300).

Diane Niebuhr and her husband, Mark, bought Hope's Bridal in 1985 and still run the business, which is known as Hope's Bridal and Prom today. While Hope's has expanded and includes a second store in Davenport, Iowa, the barn remains the hub. "Iowa Nice" customer service is the key. "We haven't lost our agricultural roots," said Niebuhr, who serves clients around the Midwest. "And yes, the barn is going to stay pink." (For the complete story about this unique barn, check out my blog at www.darcymaulsby.com.)

Just down the road, you're getting close to the iconic Youngville Café. At this point, you're 1,040 miles from Times Square in New York City and 1,905 miles from Lincoln Park in San Francisco, California. You're right where you need to be, though, if you're looking for old-school Lincoln Highway history.

Left: Located west of Cedar Rapids, Hope's Bridal and Prom has been housed in a distinctive pink barn since it opened in 1973. Diane Niebuhr and her husband, Mark, have owned and operated the business since 1985. "We haven't lost our agricultural roots," said Diane, who serves clients around the Midwest. *Courtesy of Roz Schultes.*

Below: Designed in a Tudor Revival style, the iconic Youngville Café still has the power to catch motorists' attention, just as it has since 1931, when Joe Young built the café and gas station for his daughter Elizabeth "Lizzie" Wheeler to manage. The Youngville Café reflected the new economic options available to women, thanks to the Lincoln Highway. *Author's collection.*

Designed in a Tudor Revival style, the Youngville Café still has the power to catch motorists' attention, just as it has for more than ninety years. In 1931, Joe Young, a widower in his seventies, built this destination near the present-day junction of Highway 30 and Highway 218 as a business and a home for his recently widowed daughter, Elizabeth "Lizzie" Wheeler.

Located near Watkins, the Youngville Café was a prime example of new economic options available to women, even in rural areas, thanks to the Lincoln Highway. Travelers and locals alike loved Youngville. The one-stop Youngville Café complex included a family-friendly roadside restaurant (with an eye-catching white-and-red color scheme), commercial bus stop, small cabin court for overnight lodging and Skelly filling station. Youngville was the only open-all-night fuel stop between Cedar Rapids and Tama in the 1930s. A yellowed newspaper clipping displayed in the café shows a picture of Lizzie Wheeler in a dress, smiling as she stands by the fuel pumps.

"Mrs. E. Wheeler is a real Skelly booster," the undated article noted. "She handles Skelly products 100% and sells the full line. Mrs. Wheeler has been our good Skelly dealer for the last seven years. Her station is noted for its clean, attractive appearance. She also has a small café in which she specializes in fried chicken and apple pie. A wonderful tourist trade has been built at this station, for which Mrs. Wheeler is responsible."

Back when the Youngville Café was new, it wasn't unusual to have roadhouses, cafés and service stations scattered along the Lincoln Highway throughout the area. That's what Bill Huyck told Dave Rasdal, a writer for the *Cedar Rapids Gazette*, when Rasdal interviewed the lively eighty-year-old for the article "A Slice of 1930s Life" for the May 15, 1995 edition. "Wheeler Inn used to be over there," said Huyck, as he pointed kitty-corner from the Youngville Café, across the intersections of Highways 30 and 218. "There was always a bootlegger there."

Other old-timers recalled the infamous Midway roadhouse, which was notorious for gambling, wild parties and cabins that were rented for short periods of time. Some even nicknamed the place "The Ringside," since there was a fight there about every Saturday night.

Youngville held a special place in Huyck's heart, though, because he helped build it in 1931 when he was seventeen. "It was hotter than the devil," he said. "A dry, hot summer." Huyck drove a truck to haul building supplies to the Youngville construction site, including lime from Cedar Rapids that he helped mix to make the stucco for the building. In later years, the Newhall, Iowa native stopped at the Youngville Café to eat.

"They served Sunday dinner here, and they had quite a following. They always had good pie."

Helen (Kelly) Pieper grew up on a farm east of the Youngville Café. In the early 1930s, she worked part time with Lizzie Wheeler and her daughter, Hazel, earning fifty cents per week pumping gas, cleaning, waiting tables and making beds in the Wheelers' apartment above the café. "I had to save the money," Pieper told Rasdal, who wrote up her story in "Life Was Hard in E. Iowa Growing Up Around Youngville Café," which appeared in the May 5, 2003 edition of the *Gazette*. "I remember buying shoes and dresses and things like that. You can't imagine how poor people were during the Depression."

The standard meal—roast beef, mashed potatoes and gravy, peas, a salad and coffee—sold for a quarter back then, recalled Pieper, who worked at the Youngville Café until she graduated from Newhall High School in 1941.

The Youngville Café also served as a rest stop for truck drivers and others who liked to play punch board games before the State of Iowa put a stop to games of chance. When I stopped by the Youngville Café in June 2018, a punch board hung on the wall. You could find punch boards in the United States from roughly 1900 until 1970, although they were particularly popular during the 1930s through 1950s.

A punchboard generally consists of a square piece of wood or cardboard in which hundreds of holes have been drilled and filled with slips of rolled or folded paper. Each slip of paper has a number or combination of symbols printed on it. Customers paid the punch board's operator a set amount of money (usually a nickel, dime or quarter) for a chance to use a metal stylus (or "punch") to break the seal on the hole of their choice and "punch" one of the slips of paper out of the board. If the number or symbols on the slip of paper matched one of the predetermined winning combinations, the player received a prize (typically cash).

RESTORING A SLICE OF LOCAL HISTORY

Lizzie Wheeler ran the Youngville Café for years until she retired and moved to Cedar Rapids. Her son Lester ran the Youngville Café until 1967, when it could no longer accommodate the number of cars, trucks and buses that stopped there. The main reason the Youngville Café closed permanently was that parking along Highway 30 was no longer permitted.

After the business closed, the building was rented as a living space and later "abandoned to vandals," as the *Vinton Eagle* newspaper noted in 2010. It was slated to be demolished when Highway 30 was widened. Then some locals stepped up to help preserve one of the few remaining rural filling station/eateries in Iowa.

As Iowans prepared for the sesquicentennial honoring Iowa's 150th anniversary of statehood in 1996, the Benton County Sesquicentennial Commission decided to restore the Youngville Café. Richard Grovert, Claude Conklin and Otto Hauser helped organize the Youngville Highway History Association (YHHA) around 1997, according to the article "A Story of Pie and Partnership at the Youngville Cafe," in the August 17, 2010 edition of the *Vinton Eagle*.

At that time, many folks still had a direct connection to the Youngville Café. "One fellow lived on a farm north of Van Horne, and he told me how when he was little, his grandpa would ask if wanted to go for ride," Richard Grovert said. "He always said yes because he knew they would end up at the Youngville Café for pie, but once in awhile he'd get ice cream."

Restoring the Youngville Café wasn't easy. Vandals had painted graffiti on the building, the stucco walls and the roof were in disrepair and windows were broken or gone. "There were no booths here when we started," Grovert said. Fortunately, the volunteers acquired booths from a café in Chelsea (a Lincoln Highway town in Tama County) that had closed due to massive flooding in the summer of 1993.

While the Youngville Café was closed permanently and abandoned years ago, volunteers restored the property in the 1990s and began serving meals in 2002. In the summer, volunteers (shown here in 2018) still serve lunch at the Youngville Café, which was added to the National Register of Historic Places in 2007. *Author's collection.*

The YHHA also moved three 1920s vintage cabins to the Youngville Café site to re-create the cabin court. Unfortunately, an arson fire destroyed the cabins in 2004.

Other pieces of the past endured. Before the original Lincoln Highway Association disbanded, it purchased thousands of concrete markers to honor Abraham Lincoln. In 1928, Boy Scouts placed these markers along the Lincoln Highway from coast to coast. One of those markers is displayed outside the Youngville Café.

In 2002, volunteers began serving meals at the Youngville Café, which was added to the National Register of Historic Places in 2007. The Youngville Café reopened as not only a café but also a farmers' market site and "mini museum," complete with newspaper clippings and vintage photos. One picture shows Dale and Helen Mathis by their car with the words "Just Married" on the driver's side door. They tied the knot on July 14, 1944, and stayed at one of the Youngville cabins during their honeymoon.

The Youngville Café serves lunches (including grilled cheese, loose-meat ground beef sandwiches, pork tenderloins and more) from early summer through early fall. Save room for the homemade pie. Depending on the day, you may choose from apple, cherry, blueberry, rhubarb, peach, pecan or raspberry.

Unfortunately, the Youngville Café site suffered extensive damage when a derecho (an inland hurricane) ripped across hundreds of miles in Iowa, often following the old Lincoln Highway, on August 10, 2020. (That had already been a tough year for the Youngville Café, which didn't open due to the COVID-19 pandemic.) The café did not reopen in 2021 as cleanup and recovery efforts continued. The YHHA announced on its Facebook page that it reopened the café in early June 2022 and ran it Tuesdays from 11:00 a.m. to 2:00 p.m. through September 2022.

This is good news for people like Roz Schultes of rural Templeton, Iowa, who grew up in Cedar Rapids in the 1950s and 1960s. She still travels along the Lincoln Highway when she returns to the Cedar Rapids area to visit her family and has many fond memories of the Youngville Café.

When Schultes was in grade school, her grandparents would take her and her older brother, Neil, on an outing each summer to the Meskwaki powwow in Tama. They'd stop at the Youngville Café for a meal and homemade pie. "Back then, it was a big deal to go out to eat," said Schultes, who is still a fan of chocolate pie. "I'm glad there are still so many interesting places like the Youngville Café along the Lincoln Highway."

Good Eats Abound Daily at the Lincoln Café

This is also true farther west in Belle Plaine. Drake Hokanson saw this when he was researching his book *The Lincoln Highway: Main Street Across America* in the 1980s. "Though convenience stores, car dealers and supermarkets have sprung up along the old highway through town, a slow drive and a few stops reveal much about the Lincoln in the days prior to 1936," he wrote.

His words are still true today, as I discovered during a few fun trips to Belle Plaine in the spring of 2021. A must-stop destination is the Lincoln Café, which has been serving meals since 1928. In its early days, this was a popular spot for Lincoln Highway travelers. Long after the highway was rerouted to the north, the Lincoln Café never lost its appeal. When Travel Iowa assembled the ultimate county-by-county restaurant tour in 2018, featuring one must-visit restaurant in each of Iowa's ninety-nine counties, the Lincoln Café made the list.

This is no chain restaurant. It's just like you'd imagine a classic, hometown café to be, with daily specials hand-written on a dry-erase board by the cash register. If those enticing options aren't enough to distract you, the cooler

Belle Plaine showcases its Lincoln Highway heritage on this striking mural downtown. The mural was painted around 2010 as part of Belle Plaine's role as a Main Street Iowa Community, which focuses on downtown revitalization and economic development through historic preservation. *Author's collection.*

The Lincoln Café in Belle Plaine has been serving meals since 1928, when it was popular spot for Lincoln Highway travelers. Long after the highway was rerouted to the north, the Lincoln Café never lost its appeal. *Author's collection.*

The Lincoln Café in Belle Plaine is a classic hometown café, with daily specials and a cooler filled with delectable slices of cream pies and fruit pies. *Author's collection.*

filled with delectable slices of pie certainly will. (Okay, maybe it's just me, but I'm a sucker for chocolate cream pie every time.)

When you're seated at a booth or table, you're not alone if you can't decide what you want. The Lincoln Café serves up classic comfort foods of all kinds, from homemade soups to sandwiches, salads, burgers, barbecue ribs and more. The Lincoln Café also offers breakfast all day, along with incredible broasted chicken. They prepare everything in house, and meals are cooked to order.

This family-friendly environment is definitely the kind of place that brings a community together. Notice the bulletin board by the front door, filled with homemade local advertisements for upcoming community events and other noteworthy news.

Want to learn more about Belle Plaine and the Lincoln Café? Stop by the Belle Plaine Area Museum, which is just a few blocks away from the restaurant. You can check out a vintage Lincoln Café menu (where most of the prices were less than one dollar), see an oval black-and-white plate used back in the day at the Lincoln Café and learn about the great fire of 1894, which started in a blacksmith shop where the Lincoln Café now stands.

Herring Hotel: Part Historical Treasure, Part Endangered Eyesore

Across the street from the Lincoln Café, you might notice a timeworn building. It's almost hard to believe that this nondescript building at the intersection of Eighth Avenue and Thirteenth Street was once a landmark hotel.

No one's been able to check in for years. The place is in rough shape, with sagging ceilings, old bathtubs turned sideways in former guest rooms, rotting mattresses and other debris. And yet there are many hints, like "Herring" spelled in the floor tiles, that this edifice was once extraordinary.

The Herring Hotel retains a strong sense of time and place. Will P. Herring opened the Herring Hotel, or "Herring Cottage," as it was known in its early years, in May 1900. Designed by Cedar Rapids architect Charles A. Dieman, the Herring was often advertised as "The Swellest Little Hotel in Iowa."

The Herring was strategically located within two blocks of the busy railroad depot. Herring drove a distinctive "auto bus" to the depot to pick up guests and deliver them back to the train. The Herring was also perfectly positioned for more business when the route for the new Lincoln Highway was announced in 1913.

Within months of Belle Plaine being included on the Lincoln Highway, however, a fire destroyed the Herring Hotel's attic and roof on February 11, 1914. Undeterred, Will Herring viewed this as an opportunity for growth. He added a full third story to the hotel to include more guest rooms. Some additional rearranging allowed him to install private baths in some of the guest rooms, which now numbered thirty-nine or forty. (Different articles in the *Belle Plaine Union* newspaper reported different numbers.)

As automobile traffic increased, Herring tailored his advertising and his hotel amenities to accommodate this new breed of tourist, modifying his slogan to the "Swellest Little Hotel on the Lincoln Highway." In a 1917 ad for the Herring Hotel, auto travelers were invited to "stop and knock off some of the mud or dust, as the case may be, and get a Souvenir Postal Card anyway, whether it is meal time or not. You are welcome. Rooms with baths. Cordially yours, Will P. Herring & Son."

Encouraging motorists to stay at a hotel shows how in tune Herring was with the needs of his potential customers. Hotels weren't the only places competing for travelers' business around this time. Rustic tourist camps were springing up along the Lincoln Highway, including the Way Farers Camp, which Carlos and Leonna Tippie opened in 1924 at the east edge of Belle Plaine. This was Iowa's first "cabin court," according to the Belle Plaine Area Museum, and offered lodging and other basic necessities travelers needed.

Since typical auto travelers in this era were often covered with dust or even mud, thanks to Iowa's unimproved roads, they were reluctant to stay in a hotel where they had to traipse through a fancy lobby in their grimy clothes. Herring's inviting message probably won over some tired travelers who might otherwise have settled for the less formal offerings of the nearby Way Farers camp.

Herring invested in more amenities to make the Herring Hotel even more appealing, including a steam-heated garage for guests' automobiles. What a luxury, particularly during inclement weather, to unload your car in a heated, enclosed garage directly connected to the hotel where you could comfortably spend the night.

Many well-known people stayed at the Herring Hotel, including President Theodore Roosevelt, various midwestern governors, senators, representatives and many famous speakers from the popular Chautauqua circuit, which brought culture, education and entertainment to small towns across the country in the early twentieth century.

A 1922 remodeling project made the Herring even more exceptional. The hotel boasted Craftsman-inspired design, an ornate wooden staircase from the main floor to the second floor, terrazzo floors in the lobby and a variety

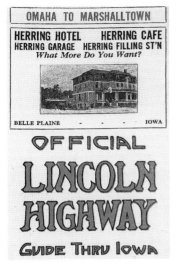

Left: The Herring Hotel, which was designed by Cedar Rapids architect Charles A. Dieman, was sometimes advertised as the "Swellest Little Hotel in Iowa." By the 1920s, it included a steam-heated garage for guests' automobiles and offered a filling station too. *Courtesy Clinton County Historical Society.*

Right: Belle Plaine–area business leaders organized the Lincoln Highway Glad Hand Club in 1925. The Glad Hand Club was like a local version of AAA, formed "for the mutual protection of the tourist," according to a 1926 Glad Hand Club brochure. *Courtesy Belle Plaine Area Museum.*

of inviting spaces where guests could gather. These included a sunroom near the lobby and two rooms off the south side of the lobby, labeled as the "parlor" and the "writing room," respectively, in the tile floors below the rooms' French doors.

By 1927, the Herring Hotel's garage area had been expanded to hold thirty cars. The garage later housed an auto sales business, including an Essex show room. Guests appreciated this level of service. Dallas Lore Sharp wrote in 1928 in his book *The Better Country*, a cross-country travel memoir, of staying overnight at the Herring Hotel with his wife, Daphne. They found Will Herring eager to please his guests.

The Herring Hotel also served as the headquarters of the Lincoln Highway Glad Hand Club, which was organized at the hotel in 1925. The Glad Hand Club was like a local version of AAA. Business proprietors who catered to the traveling public along the Lincoln Highway banded together through the Glad Hand Club "for the mutual protection of the tourist," according to a 1926 brochure from the club.

Most club members came from Belle Plaine, including cafés, filling stations, auto parts stores and hotels. The Glad Hand Club was a fairly short-lived organization, however, and disbanded by the late 1930s. This wasn't because the club hadn't been effective, but rather because big changes came to Belle Plaine, from the Herring Hotel to the Lincoln Highway.

Beginning of a Long, Slow End

By the early 1930s, plans were in the works to relocate the Lincoln Highway (now known as Highway 30) out of Belle Plaine and shift the route farther north. Many local residents were furious. "If the Iowa State Highway Commission and its chief engineer Fred White succeed in divorcing Belle Plaine from U.S. No. 30 by completing a cut-off north of this city, they at least will know they have been in a fight," stated the *Belle Plaine Union*.

Numerous articles from this period reported on U.S. Representative John Gwynne's efforts to squash this "unnecessary, money-wasting crisis," as the press called it. *Belle Plaine Union* editor O.C. Burrows drove to Washington, D.C., at the request of the Belle Plaine Commerce Club to support Iowa Congressman Gwynne's efforts.

By June 7, 1935, however, the battle was lost. "Despite the brilliance of a June day, a certain, unmistakable pall hung over Belle Plaine Friday. The Iowa State Highway Commission had taken the Lincoln Highway out of Belle Plaine," reported the *Benton County News*.

More challenges lay ahead when Will Herring passed away in 1937. While the Herring family continued to own the hotel until 1960, other people operated the business. The Herring Hotel's reputation gradually diminished, and the building showed a run-down appearance.

In the 1970s, the hotel became the Graham House, which was more of a rental property. In recent years, the hotel has stood vacant. In 2016, the Herring Hotel was included on Preservation Iowa's Most Endangered Buildings list and still faces an uncertain future.

Sankot's Garage Grew Up with the Lincoln Highway

Just down the street from the Herring Hotel is the Sankot Garage, another historic treasure that makes you feel like you've stepped back in time,

Bill Sankot (shown here in 2021) got the Sankot Motor Company (also known as the Sankot Garage) listed in the National Register of Historic Places around 1995. Sankot still likes spending time at the garage, where many of the machines, desk and more have been for decades. "It's better to wear out than rust out," he said. *Author's collection.*

especially when your tour guide is Bill Sankot, the third generation to own the business.

Originally known as the Sankot Motor Company, the company started in the early 1900s. It moved into its current location in 1927, when the attached garage was constructed, noted the article "History Tuneup: Belle Plaine Garage Earns Place in National Registry," which ran in the June 16, 1996 edition of the *Cedar Rapids Gazette.*

The Lincoln Highway passed right in front of the garage along Thirteenth Street. During the late 1920s, while he was still in high school, Bill's father, Frank "Pansy" Sankot, began working for his uncles, Charles, O.B. (Otto) and Sidney Sankot. Those were the days when travelers could dial "14" when they needed a wrecker. The Sankot Garage was open twenty-four hours a day, with the motto "We never sleep."

By the time Bill Sankot began running the place, which was listed in the National Register of Historic Places in the mid-1990s, he did a lot of tractor repair and other mechanical work. His list of Murphy's Laws is still posted

Above: The Sankot Motor Company in Belle Plaine used this self-made wrecker from a 1929 Cadillac to assist Lincoln Highway travelers (just dial "14" for service, note the business's vintage ads). The Sankot family's business was open twenty-four hours a day, with the motto "We never sleep." *Courtesy of Sankot's Garage.*

Right: In 1936, Kingfish Levinsky, a heavyweight boxer from Chicago, needed to have his vehicle towed out of the ditch near Belle Plaine. After the crew at the Sankot Motor Company helped him out, Levinsky posed for a picture before resuming his journey. *Courtesy of Sankot's Garage.*

in the shop. His favorite? "Anything you try to fix will take longer and cost more than you thought."

Now in his mid-seventies, Bill Sankot still likes spending time at the Sankot Garage, with its wooden floorboards stained with oil and machines that were first used nearly a century ago. "It's better to wear out than rust out," he said.

Preston's Station Remains a Belle Plaine Landmark

As you head west out of Belle Plaine on the old Lincoln Highway, you can't miss Preston's Station, with its riot of color from vintage metal signs for Star Tires, Texaco Motor Oil and more.

Preston's Station began in 1923 when Mary Helen Preston's great-grandfather George W. Preston purchased a Standard Oil station for $100 for his four sons to operate. The station was built by Frank Fiene in 1912, just before the Lincoln Highway was dedicated.

Preston's Station was originally located at the corner of Seventh Avenue and Nineteenth Street in Belle Plaine. "It was moved here by mules around 1927 or 1928," said Mary Helen Preston, speaking of "Preston's Corner" at the intersection of Fourth Avenue and Thirteenth Street.

While the Lincoln Highway was rerouted north of Belle Plaine in the 1930s, Preston's Station continued to operate until the late 1980s. The Prestons also ran a three-room motel they'd built in 1958 next to the station. Mary Helen's grandfather George Preston sold fuel, cigarettes, candy and pop at the station, along with basic supplies that motorists needed. "It was like a Casey's convenience store before there was Casey's," Preston said.

While George Preston stopping selling fuel in 1986, he kept the station open a few more years, since he enjoyed having adults and kids stop by. "Grandpa would 'hold court' here," said Preston, the fourth generation of her family to own the station, along with her husband, Garry. "Grandpa never met a stranger."

Folks had a lot to talk about, since George had started covering the station with a variety of old advertising and road signs in the 1970s and 1980s as a way to preserve history. "Grandpa was one of the first 'American Pickers,'" said Preston, a Kansas City native who loved visiting her Preston grandparents in Belle Plaine each summer. "He knew the value of things that other people threw away."

George eventually filled up the garage next to the filling station. "The saying, 'One man's trash is another man's treasure' holds true for both

The eye-catching Preston's Station (shown here in 2017) at the intersection of Fourth Avenue and Thirteenth Street in Belle Plaine, remains a Lincoln Highway landmark, complete with its riot of color from vintage metal signs for Star Tires, Texaco Motor Oil and more. *Author's collection.*

For decades, George Preston sold fuel, cigarettes, candy and pop at Preston's Station, along with basic supplies that motorists needed. George was well known for his storytelling skills and appeared on *The Tonight Show* with Johnny Carson in 1990. *Courtesy of Mary Helen Preston.*

Grandpa and my dad, Ronald," said Preston, president of the Iowa Lincoln Highway Association. "Trust me, nothing has been thrown out."

She's not kidding. The interior walls and shelves in Preston's Station are filled with pieces of the past, including original packets of Bower's Bigger Bug Remover Cloth (only fifty-nine cents each), vintage Iowa license plates, cardboard advertisements from the days when gasoline was twenty-one cents per gallon, a metal can of Ford Anti-Freeze priced at one dollar and boxes that once held Roi-Tan cigars, Hershey's chocolate bars with almonds and Peter Paul's Mounds candy bars, "10 cent size."

Preston's Station, which is listed in the National Register of Historic Places, seems almost frozen in time. "It's pretty much the way Grandpa left it when he closed it in 1989," said Preston, adding that the desk and chair in the station belonged to George.

When I stopped by in March 2021 to visit Mary Helen, I half expected George Preston himself to come around the corner and regale us with stories of the Lincoln Highway and Belle Plaine. "We're almost certain some of the stories are urban legends, but only Grandpa and Dad knew the truth," Preston said. "As Grandpa said many times, 'If you don't believe me, go ask Blanche,'—my grandma."

George Preston loved to chat on Iowa radio stations, from WMT in Cedar Rapids to WHO in Des Moines. In 1990, he started a 900 number that people could call to listen to his Lincoln Highway stories. His legendary storytelling even landed him an interview on *The Tonight Show* with Johnny Carson in 1990. "Grandpa would talk about anything to anyone who would listen," Preston said. "He thought Belle Plaine was the greatest little town in Iowa and loved keeping the history of the Lincoln Highway alive."

While George died in 1993, his spirit lives on at Preston's Station, which remains a prominent landmark for Belle Plaine and the Lincoln Highway. Fortunately, the station survived the derecho that ripped through the area on August 10, 2020. "That was worse than a tornado," said Preston, who noted that the storm broke one of the front windows on the station and snapped off some large tree limbs nearby.

Preston is glad that she can still show off Preston's Station, which attracts visitors across America and around the globe, from Europe to Japan. "Old places matter. To this day, I still love the smell of gasoline," said Preston, who plans on restoring the canopy that once covered the gas pumps and has thought about installing a charging station for electric vehicles. "Keeping Lincoln Highway history alive is in my blood. Garry and I are dedicated to preserving the legacy of Preston's Station and the Lincoln Highway."

TAMA COUNTY

As you leave Benton County, the landscape along the Lincoln Highway begins to change around Tama County. Parts of this area have been dubbed the "Bohemian Alps" in reference to the big hills and the Europeans who settled there in the 1800s.

The challenging terrain explains why the Lincoln Highway originally took a more southerly route in the early days through flatter, lower-lying areas around the tiny town of Chelsea. Here you're truly on the back roads, which lead to the Silver Dollar Tavern and a funeral home turned bed-and-breakfast.

A community rich in Czech heritage, Chelsea abounds with history. If you'd been here about ninety years ago, you might have met Charles Blazek and his son, George. The Blazek family expanded their restaurant (which was famous for its hamburgers) with an outdoor beer garden and dance pavilion. Countless couples danced to Bohemian music at Blazek's Park. In later years, other businesses like Ludy & Mary's Trapping Supplies Inc. attracted people to town. "The store could easily have been a trading post when such trappers as the legendary Jim Bridger made a living trapping and trading furs," noted the article "Fur Store Stirs Image of 1800s Trading Post," in the March 13, 1988 edition of the *Des Moines Register*, which featured Ludvick "Ludy" Sheda.

Unfortunately for local residents, the nearby Iowa River has long been prone to flooding. Major washouts occurred in 1918, 1947 (where thirteen

June 5, 1918 - Flood in Chelsea

The small town of Chelsea along the old Lincoln Highway is known for its Czech heritage, as well as some remarkable flooding from the nearby Iowa River. Major washouts occurred in 1918 (shown here), 1947, 1993, 2008 and 2013. *Courtesy of Belle Plaine Area Museum.*

inches of water flooded Swalm's Drug Store and other buildings), 1993, 2008 and 2013. The devastating flood of 1993 left Chelsea underwater for about thirty days and wiped out more than forty houses, according to news reports.

The 1993 tragedy also prompted an unsuccessful effort to relocate the entire town to higher ground. The proposal attracted national media attention and "forged an iron will in the 250-some residents," according to a *USA Today* article that noted the relocation plan went nowhere. "It's just another flood," one resident told the newspaper.

One place that has withstood all those floods is Periwinkle Place Manor, the former Hrabak Funeral Home. In 1892, Joseph Hrabak Sr. founded the business, which was one of the first funeral homes in Iowa. While the Hrabak-Neuhaus Funeral & Cremation Service is still in business in Belle Plaine, the Hrabak Funeral Home closed in July 2003.

The property was sold to a private homeowner who resided there until a fire nearly destroyed this beautiful piece of history. The home was abandoned until Jodi Philipp recognized its potential. "When I found her, she was black and lifeless, but I could see her grand beauty," Philipp said.

Periwinkle Place Manor in Chelsea is housed in the former Hrabak Funeral Home, which opened in 1892. In more recent years, the property (which some claim is haunted) has become one of the most unique bed-and-breakfasts in Iowa, complete with murder-mystery dinners. *Author's collection.*

Philipp and her family bought the home in 2013 and turned it into one of the most unique bed-and-breakfasts in Iowa—sometimes dubbed a "dead-and-breakfast." For starters, Periwinkle Place Manor takes its name from an antique periwinkle-colored casket that had been stored in the basement for years and remains on the property.

Then there are the murder-mystery dinners that Phillip hosts. During these events, guests can relax in the backyard by a fire pit surrounded by "couches" made from old caskets (yes, seriously). People also gather for drinks, karaoke and games in the property's coach house, which once housed the horse-drawn hearse.

So, is Periwinkle Place Manor haunted? That was my question when I stopped by for a murder-mystery dinner in March 2021. After all, many souls have passed through this former funeral home dating back to the 1800s, and I'd heard strange stories. During my visit, I sat by the periwinkle casket. I toured the house. I experienced nothing out of the ordinary.

Yet a number of guests have reported all kinds of unusual activity, from a rocking horse rocking for no apparent reason, old dolls moving (with no human intervention), doors opening and closing on their own, humming, eerie footsteps and even ghost sightings. "Come for a visit and see for yourself," Phillip said.

KING TOWER CREATED MODERN TRUCK STOP IN 1937

If you survive any hauntings in Chelsea, your next stop is Tama. As you drive along the old Lincoln Highway into town from the east, there's an interesting-looking place down the road from the Tama Livestock Auction. While you can't eat at King Tower anymore, you can tell by looking at the shuttered building that this place was something unique.

This was a forerunner of today's truck stops. When W.W. Mansfield opened King Tower in October 1937, it was called central Iowa's most modern one-stop station, complete with a two-story restaurant (including sleeping rooms on the second floor for restaurant employees). "The restaurant will cater to Sunday dinners, as well as regular meals throughout

Opened in 1937, King Tower in Tama along the Lincoln Highway was called central Iowa's most modern one-stop destination for Lincoln Highway travelers. It boasted a large concrete driveway for easy access, a garage and service station that offered twenty-four-hour service and a popular restaurant. *Author's collection.*

Comfort foods from sandwiches to homemade soup filled the menu at the King Tower Café, where custom murals in the dining room celebrated Tama County's rich Meskwaki Indian history. A devastating derecho that hit the area in August 2020 prompted the owners to permanently close the café. *Author's collection.*

the week," noted a *Tama News-Herald* newspaper article from October 28, 1937. "Other features planned on the menu include deep-fat-fried chicken, barbecued ribs and special sandwiches."

King Tower, which boasted a large, concrete driveway for easy access, also included a garage and service station with twenty-four-hour service. "The garage building is 40 by 50 feet and built so even the largest trucks may drive through the building, eliminating backing and turning," noted the 1937 newspaper article "King Tower Café Makes Debut to Motorists." "Neon signs will flash a welcome to motorists over one-half mile distant."

The second floor of the garage was equipped with showers and sleeping accommodations for truckers. Future plans for King Tower, which was located on fifteen acres, called for cabins and a trailer camp to be built at the back of the property.

For generations, King Tower was a place where travelers and locals alike enjoyed hearty meals and slices of pie. My mom and I stopped here for lunch on Saturday, August 8, 2020. We had planned to attend the annual powwow at the nearby Meskwaki Settlement, but the event was canceled due to COVID-19. We could still enjoy the café's custom murals celebrating Tama County's rich Meskwaki Indian history.

I also enjoyed a fantastic bowl of soup with my sandwich. None of us during the busy lunch crowd that day had any idea these would be among the last meals served at King Tower Café, which had been included in the National Register of Historic Places in early 2020.

A devastating derecho (an inland hurricane) tore through the area on Monday, August 10, 2020. On August 18, 2020, the *Tama Toledo News* reported that "Historic King Tower Won't Reopen," after owners Jimmy and Lejka Arifi announced on their Facebook social media page that they planned to shut their doors for good. The combination of the COVID-19 lockdowns and the derecho proved overwhelming. "We have had many great times at King Tower, and we leave with many treasured memories," wrote the Arifi family on Facebook. "Stay strong, Iowa."

While I didn't get the recipe for the soup I ate that day at the King Tower Café, I re-created my own version. Enjoy!

Simple Beef Orzo Soup

2 tablespoons extra virgin olive oil
1 yellow onion, chopped
3 carrots, sliced
3 celery stalks, diced
1 pound ground beef
3 garlic cloves, minced
Salt and pepper, to taste
1 teaspoon paprika
1 (28-ounce) can diced tomatoes
Vegetable or chicken broth, approximately 5 to 6 cups
½ cup uncooked orzo pasta
Handful chopped fresh parsley and/or fennel fronds, to taste

In a cooking pot, heat 2 tablespoons extra virgin olive oil until shimmering. Add onions, carrots and celery. Cook for 3 to 4 minutes, stirring regularly, until softened. Add ground beef and minced garlic. Season with salt, pepper and paprika. Cook on medium-high, stirring regularly, until meat is fully browned. (Drain any excess grease and return pot to the heat). Add diced tomatoes and broth. Bring to a boil and then lower heat and simmer for 10 minutes. Add orzo and raise the heat to medium-high. Place the lid on the pot, leaving it somewhat open. Cook orzo to al dente (about 8 to 10 minutes). Remove from heat and stir in fresh parsley and fennel. Taste and adjust seasoning to your liking.

EXPLORE TAMA'S FAMOUS 1915 LINCOLN HIGHWAY BRIDGE

Sometimes failure and triumph are intertwined in pieces of the past, like the twenty-two-foot-long Lincoln Highway Bridge that spans Mud Creek in Tama, just down the road from King Tower.

The bridge's story began on May 17, 1915, when the Tama County Board of Supervisors hired Paul Kingsley, a relatively new contractor from Strawberry Point, Iowa, to build fifty-three bridges and culverts throughout the county. Kingsley agreed to complete the work by November 1, 1915, for $39,900. (That's more than $1.1 million in 2022 dollars.) When the deadline arrived, however, he'd only completed a fraction of this ambitious project, according to the Iowa Department of Transportation.

While supervisors declared Kingsley in default of the contract by 1916 and hired other firms to complete the work, Kingsley did leave a lasting legacy that included the Lincoln Highway Bridge, which he constructed in 1915. The county supervisors opted to add architectural expression to the

Constructed in 1915, the guard rails on this distinctive bridge at Tama spell the name "Lincoln Highway" on both sides, making the bridge an early advertisement for the Lincoln Highway. *Courtesy of Lincoln Highway Museum.*

otherwise typical concrete slab structure to distinguish the bridge from the hundreds of others along the route. Guard rails spelling the name "Lincoln Highway" on both sides of this bridge showcased this structure as an early advertisement for the Lincoln Highway.

The bridge symbolized a new era of progress for Tama County. When the route of the transcontinental Lincoln Highway was first established in 1913, the citizens of Tama and surrounding areas immediately recognized its importance. "We can scarcely estimate the travel this national road will induce," the *Traer Star-Clipper* newspaper reported in November 1913. "This will probably become the best long-distance auto road in the United States. Fortunate indeed is Tama County to have it pass through her entire length."

Tama's Lincoln Highway bridge was listed in the National Register of Historic Places in 1978. Community donations paid for the restoration of the bridge in 1987. Motorists today can travel the original route of the Lincoln Highway in the Tama area by following the signs that begin at the Lincoln Highway Bridge and continue west on Fifth Street. The bridge "stands as a dramatic reminder of a time when few roads were paved, and the campaign to 'get out of the mud' had just begun," notes an elegant metal plaque near the Lincoln Highway Bridge Park.

As you explore the Tama area, you're near the Meskwaki Nation. Members of the Sac and Fox Tribe of the Mississippi in Iowa, or "People of the Red Earth," have called this area home since the 1700s. For more than one hundred years, Meskwaki Nation residents have celebrated their annual powwow. Held in August, this powwow is the only one of its kind in Iowa and features dancing, singing, handcrafts, food, games and fun.

When Roz Schultes was growing up in Cedar Rapids, her grandparents would take her and her older brother, Neil, on an outing each summer to Tama to the Meskwaki powwow, which attracted big crowds. "We looked forward to it," Schultes said. "I was so impressed to see real Indians in their ceremonial outfits with feathers and beautiful colors."

Since the 1990s, countless visitors have also connected with the Meskwaki Nation by visiting the Meskwaki Bingo Casino Hotel. The casino includes a mini-museum dedicated to the history of the Meskwakis. You can also visit the Meskwaki Cultural Center and Museum just down the road, especially if you'd like to learn about the remarkable Meskwaki Code Talkers of World War II.

Twenty-seven Meskwakis enlisted in the Iowa National Guard in 1941. Eight were chosen for special instruction in machine gunnery and radio communications operation. During World War II, they used a code based on

For more than a century, this bridge at Tama has been one of the most iconic landmarks along the entire Lincoln Highway in America. The bridge was listed in the National Register of Historic Places in 1978. A small park nearby details local Lincoln Highway history. *Author's collection.*

Since it opened in the 1990s, the Meskwaki Bingo Casino Hotel (shown here in 2018) has welcomed countless visitors. The casino includes a mini-museum dedicated to sharing the history of the Meskwaki tribe. *Author's collection.*

American Indian languages to send secret messages about troop movements, battlefield tactics and directions for artillery fire.

The Meskwaki code talkers were assigned to the Thirty-Fourth Red Bull division. The code talkers' duties placed them in great peril, however, when they were deployed to the deserts of North Africa, a region Meskwaki Frank Sanache described as "the worst place this side of hell." Italian soldiers captured Sanache in Tunisia in 1943, while the German military captured Dewey Youngbear and Judy Wayne Wabaunasee.

While all the Meskwaki code talkers survived the war, their remarkable story faded into history until Robin Roberts spearheaded a campaign to help the code talkers receive Congressional Gold Medals for their military service. "Who knows how many lives they saved by using the Meskwaki language to communicate vital military messages?" said Roberts, whose uncle Dewey Roberts served as a Meskwaki code talker.

The Meskwaki Cultural Center and Museum at Tama preserves the remarkable story of the Meskwaki code talkers. During World War II, these members of the U.S. military used a code based on American Indian languages to send secret messages about troop movements, battlefield tactics and directions for artillery fire. *Courtesy of Meskwaki Cultural Center and Museum.*

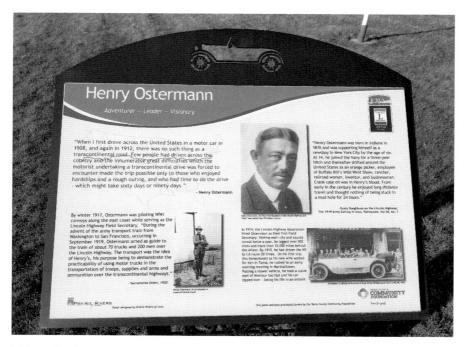

This marker in Montour honors Henry Ostermann, the first field secretary of the Lincoln Highway Association. Before he was killed in an automobile accident as he headed to Marshalltown in 1920, Ostermann had made twenty cross-county trips on the Lincoln Highway and had traveled with the U.S. Army convoy over the Lincoln Highway in 1919. *Author's collection.*

Iowa senator Charles Grassley presented Congressional Gold Medals to the code talkers' families at a ceremony in Washington, D.C., in 2013. "These brave people put their lives in harm's way for their country, and their sacrifices should not be forgotten," he said.

There are many sacrifices that should not be forgotten. You're reminded of this when you drive through the tiny town of Montour along the Lincoln Highway. At the Maple Hill Cemetery, a historical marker unveiled in 2019 honors Henry Ostermann, the first field secretary of the Lincoln Highway Association. On the early morning of June 7, 1920, Ostermann headed west on the Lincoln Highway in his 1918 Packard Twin Six white touring car. The newlywed knew the highway well, since he had made twenty cross-county trips and guided the 1919 U.S. Army convoy over the Lincoln Highway from coast to coast.

On this June day, Ostermann was headed to a meeting in Marshalltown, where his wife would join him later. In his haste, he passed a slower motorist on a Lincoln Highway curve east of Montour, lost control of his vehicle and was killed instantly.

In the early days of the Lincoln Highway, Montour was a farming community. This is still true today. As you drive into town, you'll notice cattle grazing on local farms. For decades, beef lovers far and wide have flocked to downtown Montour to grill their own steaks at Rube's Steakhouse. It all started in 1973 when Glen "Rube" Rubenbauer opened a tavern here. His philosophy? Allow guests the experience of grilling generously portioned, hand-cut premium steaks over an indoor, open-hearth grill.

Word of this grill-your-own steakhouse spread fast, and people couldn't get enough of these juicy, flavorful steaks. Nearly fifty years later, Rube's Steakhouse is still inspiring social connections around the open-hearth grill. I admit, it's fun to grill your own steak and vegetables, just the way you like them, and then head back to your table to dig in.

"Most importantly, premium corn-fed steak is still at the heart of it all," notes Rube's website. "Through a partnership with Iowa Premium, every steak we serve supports local family farmers raising black Angus within 150 miles of our steakhouse. Come taste the very best beef Iowa has to offer."

MARSHALL COUNTY

Sometimes the most unlikely stories crop up in the most unlikely places along the Lincoln Highway in Iowa. As you head toward Le Grand in Marshall County, it's hard to imagine that a shallow, inland ocean filled with graceful sea creatures once covered this region of the North American landscape millions of years ago.

As those sea creatures died, they drifted into a shallow depression in the sea floor, where they were quickly buried by fine-grained lime mud. Over time, the mud turned into limestone. In the process, some of the sea creatures turned into fossils, especially in eastern Marshall County.

The Le Grand area proved to be an especially rich source of well-defined fossils. These fossil beds were exposed along the nearby Iowa River, according to the 1962 book *Crinoid and Starfish Fossils from Le Grand, Iowa* by Richard Boyt.

Settlers began mining for limestone in this area in the 1850s. Limestone was needed for building construction, ballast in railroad beds, agricultural lime for crop production and later for road gravel, which was important to the Lincoln Highway. While some of the highest-quality Le Grand limestone was used to construct the Marshall County Courthouse, the Marshalltown Public Library, the old State Historical Building in Des Moines and other buildings in central Iowa, the best treasures from the Le Grand quarry were the fossils.

Miners had discovered the first major "nest" of fossils in a limestone quarry about a mile north of Le Grand in 1874, according to "Iowa's Self-Trained Paleontologists," which appeared in the *Proceedings of the Iowa Academy of Science* in 1983. These fossils were nearly depleted by 1890,

Le Grand–area farmer Burnice "Burnie" Beane became a world-renowned amateur paleontologist by excavating and studying fossils, primarily crinoids (sometimes called "sea lilies"), from a stone quarry near Le Grand. His most remarkable discovery occurred in 1931, when he found a stone slab loaded with rare, exquisite starfish. *Courtesy of Le Grand Pioneer Heritage Library.*

however, just as a local farm boy named Burnice "Burnie" Beane (1879–1966) was discovering the joys of paleontology (the study of the history of life on Earth, based on fossils).

Beane was especially interested in crinoids, which abounded in the Le Grand area. Many of these ancient treasures could have been destroyed if Beane hadn't intervened and collected these specimens, which are displayed at the Le Grand Public Library, as well as museums around the Midwest and beyond.

What's a crinoid, you ask? They look like plants and are sometimes called "sea lilies," although they are technically echinoderms related to starfish and sea urchins. Only a few places in the world (including sites in Indiana, Montana and Germany) have yielded ancient crinoids as well preserved as those from the Le Grand quarry, according to "Underwater Iowa: Where Graceful Crinoids Once Swayed in Ancient Seas," from the spring 1995 issue of *The Palimpsest*, a journal of Iowa history.

The intricate preserved crinoids fascinated young Beane. The son of a Quaker minister, Beane had no formal training in paleontology or geology. Beane grew up on a farm adjacent to a quarry near Le Grand. In those days, amateur and professional paleontologists flocked to the Le Grand quarry to search for crinoids. "Those scientists were the idols of my boyhood," said Beane, who recalled dishes rattling in his family's farmhouse during blasting at the nearby quarry. "I pestered them with endless questions, and they answered me with inexhaustible patience. I soon became a fossil collector and spent most of my spare time at the quarry."

Even after he started a family and operated his farm, Beane's enthusiasm for hunting fossils never waned. Beane made friends among the quarry workers, who notified him when they came across anything interesting. In the summer of 1931, blasting uncovered some new fossil nests, including one about one hundred feet from the 1874 discovery. As Beane examined the exceptional level of preservation of the newly found crinoids, he made an even greater discovery: a slab loaded with rare, exquisite starfish.

Beane worked diligently to save these large, fossil-bearing slabs from the quarry's rock crusher. Word spread quickly of this remarkable fossil find in the 650-pound slab. When he saw them, Dr. Abram O. Thomas, a professor of geology at the University of Iowa, threw up his hands in amazement, Boyt wrote. "Good Lord, Mr. Beane! Where did you find them?" Thomas exclaimed. "They're worth more than the whole quarry!"

The fossils' degree of preservation prompted Dr. Charles Schuchert, a renowned paleontologist from Yale University, to call this the greatest find of fossil starfish in all of paleontology.

Exposing the fossils clearly took years of slow, painstaking work after Beane transported the choice slabs to his backyard workshop. Using dental tools, a small hammer, a toothbrush and a needle, he worked off and on for twenty-six years to prepare his great starfish slab, which contained 183 specimens.

Beane's home was packed with crinoid fossils he had collected, from large slabs to tiny specimens. Remarkably, forty new crinoid species were recovered from the Le Grand quarry through the years, and Beane discovered eleven of them. *Rhodocrinites beanei* from the Le Grand quarry was named in Beane's honor.

Beane became known internationally for his significant contributions to paleontology research, particularly fossils from the Paleozoic era. When Beane died in 1966 at age eighty-six, he was buried in the Friends' Cemetery in Marshall County. "I remember standing beside the coffin with my dad," wrote his granddaughter Karen Beane Norstrud in "Crinoids in the Sugar Bowl: Remembering My Grandfather, Amateur Paleontologist B.H. Beane," which appeared in the spring 1995 edition of *The Palimpsest*. "All his life, he had seen Grandpa surrounded by fossils. Now in a final act of farewell, Dad quietly slipped a tiny, single crinoid under Grandpa's hand."

Mining continues to this day in the Le Grand area. You can see a display a Beane's fascinating fossil research at the Le Grand Pioneer Heritage Library, which is located near the Lincoln Highway.

Missing Monet Turned Up in Marshall County Mailbox

A much different find than fossils put Le Grand and Marshall County on the map in the late 1980s. It started in Marshalltown on Thursday, March 19, 1987. As a theater group rehearsed in the Fisher Community Center, a thief entered the building around 10:00 p.m. through the main doors and headed to the foyer. He cut a painting by famed French impressionist Claude Monet out of its frame and disappeared with the painting, which was valued at $175,000 (more than $437,000 in 2022 dollars) by the St. Paul Fire and Marine Insurance Company.

The painting, *Les Bargues Depeche Devant Les Falaises D'Etretat* (*The Fishing Boats in Front of the Cliffs at Etretat*), was on loan to the chamber of commerce, reported the Associated Press (AP) in the article "Monet Painting Stolen from Community Center," which ran in newspapers nationwide on March 20, 1987.

The artwork, painted by Monet around 1891, was connected to an alarm at the police station. Police arrived at 10:09 p.m. on March 19—within minutes of the theft—but the suspect was gone, according to Police Chief James Wilkinson. The painting had hung in the community center for twenty-nine years, added Steve Ward, who was the executive vice-president of the chamber of commerce at the time. "We're shocked," Ward told the AP. "It kind of blows the socks right off you."

Robert Christensen, the building's custodian, saw the thief use a knife to remove the canvas, which measured twenty-three and five-eighth inches long and thirty-two and one-fourth inches wide. Christensen described the man as six-foot-two or six-foot-three and weighing between 230 pounds and 260 pounds. Christensen yelled at the man, who made a final slash and ran off with the painting.

The artwork was part of a collection owned by the Fisher Foundation, whose chairman, J.W. "Bill" Fisher, was a patron of the arts and former president of Fisher Controls in Marshalltown. The collection also included works by Henri Matisse and Edgar Degas. Peg Buckley, a librarian at the Des Moines Art Center, told the AP, "Whoever stole that will never get rid of it. It's extremely valuable…and any art museum would know it was stolen."

Local police, the FBI and the international police agency Interpol searched for the oil painting but came up empty. Almost a year after the crime, however, the missing Monet made national headlines once again.

Charles Polley, who was the postmaster in Le Grand at the time, found the painting on Tuesday morning, March 8, 1988, in a mail drop-off box. The painting was rolled up and bound by two rubber bands when Polley found it mixed in with other pieces of mail. He said it was dropped sometime after 3:00 p.m. Monday and before 7:30 a.m. Tuesday when he opened the mailbox. "I thought it was trash at first—but it sure wasn't trash," he told the AP. "It had the look of canvas, and I looked at the edges and knew exactly what it was. You never know what a day will bring."

GOOD EATS ABOUND IN MARSHALLTOWN

While you never know what you'll find along the Lincoln Highway, you never know what you'll see either. Shady Oaks Campground, located near the banks of Brush Creek between Le Grand and Marshalltown, has served highway travelers since the 1920s.

This is regarded by many as the first cabin camp opened on the Lincoln Highway in Iowa, according to Michael Wallis in his book *The Lincoln Highway: The Great American Road Trip.* "That was in 1925, when the campsite—including 18 cabins, a gas station, restaurant and grocery—opened in a grove of ancient bur oaks. The stand of trees had been a resting place for Indians, trappers and early settlers."

While the restaurant is gone, people still recall the restaurant's great food. "They had the best onion rings around," said Becky Merrill, a Marshalltown native who ate there in the 1960s.

This area is also the home of the Big Treehouse. Constructed by Mick Jurgensen, the Big Treehouse began in 1983. This twelve-level masterpiece is more than fifty-five feet high, with five thousand-plus square feet of floor space, electricity, some appliances, running water, porch swings and more, according to www.bigtreehouse.net.

Getting hungry? Head up to Marshalltown. Whether you want casual meal options, ethnic cuisine (from Mexican to Jack's Pho House), this county-seat town serves up global flavors accented with midwestern flair daily.

Marshalltown is also the home of upscale dining, thanks to The Tremont. The Tremont building has been a downtown Marshalltown landmark since 1874. This Main Street anchor now boasts a boutique hotel, along with two restaurants. The Tremont on Main (22 West Main Street) serves classic American food with fresh, local ingredients. The Tremont Grille (26 West Main Street) offers an Italian-style bistro serving breakfast and lunch, along

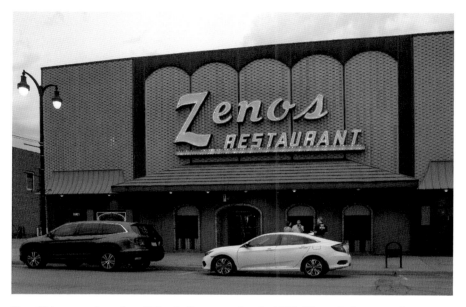

Two Chicagoans introduced Marshalltown to pizza in 1952. Through the years, the restaurant has had a few different owners, but it has been Zeno's for decades now. People still love this classic, local pizzeria. *Author's collection.*

with gourmet coffee, espresso and more. After dinner, retire upstairs to the exclusive Tremont Inn for overnight lodging with unique décor.

If you're craving pizza, head over to Zeno's (109–111 East Main Steet). Pizza was first introduced to Marshalltown by two Chicagoans: Cosmos Nigrelli and his brother-in-law, Joe Liberio, in 1952. The restaurant has had a few different names and owners through the years, but it has been Zeno's for decades now, a local classic.

If you'd rather have a burger, check out the Flying Elbow (229 North Thirteenth Street), which won Iowa's Best Burger contest in May 2022. One of its best-selling burgers is the "Real American," which is named after Hulk Hogan's theme song and reflects restaurant owner Garrett Goodman's take on the classic cheeseburger, complete with ketchup, mustard, pickles and grilled, minced onions.

"I didn't want to be a niche establishment for adventurous foodies," said Goodman, a Marshalltown native who started with a food truck and expanded to a brick-and-mortar restaurant that has survived a tornado in 2018 and the COVID-19 pandemic in 2020. "I wanted to create a place that everybody could eat at. I've always had a little bit of something for everyone."

In June 2022, the Flying Elbow celebrated a national victory with "The Tombstone," which beat a burger from the Ale 'n' Angus Pub in New York in another best-burger contest. The Tombstone is a smashburger made from a blend of chuck, brisket, short rib and Wagyu beef, topped with Manchego cheese and more.

If you want another beefy taste of Iowa, try Taylor's Maid-Rite. Located at 106 South Third Avenue, this third-generation business has been serving central Iowa for more than ninety years. Cliff Taylor purchased the 1928 franchise for $300. After Cliff passed away in 1944, his son, Don, continued to run the restaurant. In 1958, he built a state-of-the-art Maid-Rite restaurant across the street from the original location, outfitting the new store with all stainless steel equipment and two cash registers.

While various generations of the family have operated the business since then, the restaurant retains its 1950s feel, and the Maid-Rite recipe hasn't changed in ninety years. "There is no recipe," said Sandy Taylor Short, whose grandfather opened the restaurant. "We buy good beef, bone-in meat and grind it every day."

Good beef means "chuck choice or better," Short told the Marshalltown *Times Republican* in 2018. Customers are grateful that Taylor's Maid-Rite was

If you want a unique taste of Iowa, try Taylor's Maid-Rite in Marshalltown. This third-generation business has been serving loose-meat sandwiches and more since Cliff Taylor purchased the 1928 franchise for $300. In recent years, the restaurant survived a devastating tornado. *Author's collection.*

spared when a devastating tornado tore through Marshalltown on July 19, 2018. "The day after the tornado, we had calls from California, Florida and all over—making sure we were still open," Short said.

While Taylor's Maid-Rite still delights customers, another classic Marshalltown restaurant has passed into history. For generations, people loved to dine at Stone's Restaurant. Located near the railroad tracks "under the viaduct," the restaurant started in 1887. When the *Des Moines Register* ran a 2003 feature story on the iconic eatery, Stone's famous Mile High Lemon Chiffon Pie received top billing. Within a few years, however, the restaurant was gone forever, closing permanently in 2007.

You can still find recipes that claim to re-create the taste of that famous Mile High Lemon Chiffon Pie. Here's one that was shared with me.

Mile High Lemon Chiffon Pie

8 egg yolks, slightly beaten
2 cups sugar
Juice of 2 lemons
2 lemon rinds, grated
Salt to taste
2 tablespoons unflavored gelatin
½ cup cold water
8 egg whites

Cook egg yolks, 1 cup of sugar, lemon juice, lemon rinds and salt in double boiler, stirring frequently until consistency of thick custard. Soak gelatin in cold water until dissolved. Add gelatin mixture to hot custard and cool. Beat egg whites stiff but not dry. Beat in remaining cup of sugar gradually and then beat again. Fold cooled custard into beaten egg whites. Put in baked pie shell and chill three hours. Serve with whipped cream.

DAYS OF BARNS AND ROSES IN STATE CENTER

As you head west on your Lincoln Highway journey from Marshalltown, you'll reach State Center, the "Rose Capital of Iowa." Each year during the third weekend in June, the town celebrates the Rose Festival, which has been

State Center, which is known as the "Rose Capital of Iowa," celebrates the annual Rose Festival each June. You can also visit State Center's beautiful landscaped rose garden in the heart of town. *Author's collection.*

held annually since 1958 (although the event was canceled in 2020 due to COVID-19).

Even if you're not in town during the Rose Festival, you can visit State Center's beautiful landscaped garden, where residents have spent decades nurturing and showcasing many varieties of roses, old and new. Also take note of the 1932 Home Oil Gas Station (144 Fourth Street Southeast), which now houses the State Center Police Department.

Head uptown to check out Watson's Grocery at 106 West Main Street. The interior of the building, constructed in 1895, remained nearly unchanged throughout its years of operation as a grocery store. In 1981, Florence Watson closed the store, locked the doors and left everything as it was. After Florence died in 1989, the community of State Center reopened Watson's Grocery Store as an early twentieth-century grocery store museum. The property has been listed in the National Register of Historic Places since 1998.

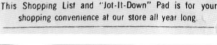

Right: Watson's Grocery in State Center was a grocery store from the time it was built in 1895 until Florence Watson closed the store for the final time in 1981, leaving everything as it was. Watson's Grocery Store is now an early twentieth-century grocery store museum. *Courtesy of Watson's Grocery.*

Below: The Pfantz family's barn in State Center is an architectural marvel. It was built in 1902 for August Riemenschneider, who became one of the best-known livestock buyers in central Iowa. The barn has been restored and is featured on the Iowa Barn Foundation tour. *Author's collection.*

Another noteworthy State Center property that's almost as old as Watson's Grocery is the Pfantz barn on the east edge of town. This stunning, four-gabled red barn, which has been called the most beautiful barn in Iowa, has been showcased in a P. Buckley Moss art print. It was even featured in *Cora Unashamed*, which *Masterpiece Theatre* filmed in the fall of 1999.

I was as captivated as others who love this barn when I stopped by in September 2017 during the Iowa Barn Foundation's annual tour of barns across Iowa. The Pfantz family's barn is an architectural marvel, rising nearly forty-eight feet at its highest point. As far as Craig Pfantz can tell, a local German carpenter built the barn in 1902 for Pfantz's great-grandfather August Riemenschneider. Mr. Riemenschneider was a German immigrant who settled in the late 1860s in State Center, where he became one of the best-known livestock buyers in central Iowa. His livestock buying station was located just down the hill from his acreage on Fourth Avenue Northeast.

Riemenschneider's business was so successful that in 1905 he built a grand, Queen Anne–style Victorian home west of the barn. He lived here until he passed away in 1916. The property had various owners through the years until Pfantz and his wife bought the acreage in 1994.

After completing some major repairs on the house, the couple turned their attention to the barn. "It was in really bad shape," said Pfantz, who noted that the barn housed an antique shop in the late 1970s and early 1980s. The Pfantz family spent more than six years restoring the barn, starting in 2001. "The barn is a living museum," said Pfantz, who has served on the Iowa Barn Foundation board. "Since so many barns are being torn down, the ones that are saved will be even more treasured."

STORY COUNTY

As you cruise past farms and barns on your way to Story County, you might notice signs pointing to the historic Reed/Niland Corner, a unique place that retains its authentic Lincoln Highway spirit. Located at the intersection of the Lincoln Highway and the Jefferson Highway (which runs from Winnipeg, Canada, to New Orleans, Louisiana), the Reed/Niland Corner started in the 1920s. It provided the perfect location for weary travelers to fill up their vehicle with gasoline, enjoy a home-cooked meal at the café and enjoy a good night's sleep, starting with a cabin court that evolved in the 1940s into one of Iowa's first "modern" motels.

"For a few years, the café was the only twenty-four-hour operation around," recalled Joan Niland, whose family used to run the business. "The employees would always joke that we never had a key for the front door."

With the motto "A good place to eat, where friends meet," the business catered to both travelers and locals. In an era when meals were breakfast, dinner and supper (not breakfast, lunch and dinner), the café served up specials including chicken and noodles, salmon loaf and minute steak, as well as menu standards like homemade bean soup.

Generations of locals, including high school athletes and fans, loved to stop at Niland's Café after games. While the café has struggled in recent years to stay in business, it's open again (as of the summer of 2022), the fresh-baked pie is back and the memories live on. "In this business, the best memories are the people you meet along the way," Joan Niland said.

The historic Reed/Niland Corner at Colo got its start in the 1920s with a filling station, café (shown here in 2016) and cabin court that evolved in the 1940s into one of Iowa's first "modern" motels. The buildings that remain retain much of their original Lincoln Highway spirit. *Author's collection.*

CHARLIE GOOD CHAMPIONS HOME-GROWN BIOFUELS

While the gas pumps at the Reed/Niland corner have been empty for years, you can fill up in Nevada. If you pull into the Good & Quick convenience store on the Lincoln Highway near downtown Nevada, you'll see a lot of ethanol fuel blends. Owner Charlie Good is happy to help you make sense of all those options.

"I don't get tired of debunking the lies about ethanol," said Good, who sells thousands of gallons of ethanol blends each year. "The truth never gets old."

It's hard to argue with Good, an ASE certified mechanic and business owner with forty years of experience. His station offers a variety of ethanol options, including E10, E20, E30 and E85 (the number reflects what percent of the gasoline is ethanol). While people are sometimes concerned that ethanol will cause engine problems, Good hasn't any complaints. "There's absolutely no downside in my book."

Above: Travelers arriving in Nevada on the Lincoln Highway are greeted with an image of Abraham Lincoln himself on this stone marker at the east edge of town. *Author's collection.*

Left: The locally owned Good & Quick convenience store near downtown Nevada offers motorists many ethanol fuel blends. These gasoline blends are made from Iowa corn. *Author's collection.*

"FIVE AND DIME" LIVES ON AT BEN FRANKLIN

If you've ever shopped at a Walmart store or a Michael's craft store, you've experienced the legacy of the beloved Ben Franklin dime stores that used to be a Main Street destination in small towns across America. You can still shop at the Ben Franklin store (1038 Sixth Street) in Nevada, a town known for its Lincoln Highway Days celebration.

The store includes eight thousand square feet filled with small and large treasures. "We are your classic five and dime with a modern twist," states the Nevada Ben Franklin's Facebook page. The store offers gifts and collectables, craft supplies, fabric, stationery, jewelry, hardware, housewares, scarves, candy, greeting cards, toys and much more.

Ben Franklin stores began popping up across America in 1927. During the golden age of American dime-store retailing, the Ben Franklin empire once totaled 2,500 stores. It influenced the career path of more than one industry disruptor. Sam and Helen Walton bought their first Ben Franklin variety store in Newport, Arkansas, in 1945. Within five years, their store became the top Ben Franklin franchise in the state and fueled bigger dreams that would lead to the creation of Walmart. Decades later

Small-town Americana lives on at the Ben Franklin store in downtown Nevada. "We are your classic five and dime with a modern twist," states the store's Facebook page. The store offers craft supplies, fabric, stationery, housewares, candy, greeting cards, toys and more. *Author's collection.*

Above: Starbuck's Drive In, located along the Lincoln Highway, has been a popular destination in Nevada for years. Customers love the burgers, onion rings, cheese balls, ice cream, pie and Starbuck's famous homemade, breaded pork tenderloin sandwiches. *Author's collection.*

Right: Lincoln Highway heritage shows up in variety of ways in Nevada, which debuted its annual Lincoln Highway Days summer celebration in 1984. This home along the Lincoln Highway honors Abraham Lincoln with a carved tree trunk in the front yard. *Author's collection.*

in Texas, Michael Dupey converted a Ben Franklin store around 1973 to start the Michael's chain.

Ironically, those larger, modern chain stores ultimately spelled doom for hundreds of small-town Ben Franklin stores. By the 1990s, as big-box stores spread across America, Ben Franklin stores started going out of business. Fortunately, there are still a handful of Ben Franklin stores around Iowa, including the one in Nevada.

Van Harden, a longtime Iowa radio broadcaster from Adel, Iowa, has long been a fan of Ben Franklin stores. "I grew up one block from a Ben Franklin store and always loved riding my bike there just to look around, or maybe spend my allowance on a model-car kit."

Ben Franklin's offer small-town charm, he added. "My wife and I have look for Ben Franklin stores when we travel. We always stop in and have a good chat with the owners."

The Ben Franklin store in Nevada celebrates its small-town heritage. "Fifty years ago, Fred & Vi Samuelson purchased the Ben Franklin Store," noted one of the store's 2021 Facebook posts. "Fred and Vi moved to Nevada, where they would raise two boys, Jimmy and Mickey. They worked endless hours and countless days to make Ben Franklin a success. Both Fred and Vi believed in supporting their community, its people, and most of all education. The gifts they've given this community have been quiet acts of kindness and love."

ANITA KING CONQUERED THE CONTINENT IN A KISSEL KAR

As you leave Nevada and cruise over to Ames, you're on the same route that a rising Hollywood star named Anita King traveled in 1915. Like many early road trips across the country, King's 1915 journey began with a bet.

William Wadsworth Hodkinson, cofounder of Paramount Pictures Corporation, offered to give King, thirty-one, a starring role in a future film production if she successfully made the unaccompanied trip via automobile. "She was already an accomplished race car driver, film stunt driver and movie actress, so she jumped at the chance," noted the article "Silent Movie Star Takes Many Detours Along Her Lincoln Highway Journey" in the fall 2020 edition of *Lincoln Highway Forum* magazine.

She received a six-cylinder Kissel Kar and an advertising sponsorship from Firestone Tires. Overnight, she became the "Paramount Girl," with

Hollywood star Anita King rolled into Ames in late September 1915 as she made a cross-country tour on the Lincoln Highway by herself. When she arrived at the Princess Theater, many people flocked to see her and her six-cylinder Kissel Kar. *Courtesy of Ames History Museum.*

the support of the film corporation publicity machine sending her off across the continent.

King rolled into Ames in late September 1915. When King stopped her car in front of the Princess Theater, people couldn't wait to see the star and her car. "She talks most entertainingly and made many friends during the short time she was here," noted the *Ames Evening Times*. "With everyone paying Miss King all the honor possible, it remained for the former mayor, J.G. Tilden, to pay her the greatest and final one just before she departed. Mr. Tilden did not get to have his picture taken with her, so they went across the street to a refreshment parlor and drank root beer together. He then presented her with three Ames pennants."

Within a few days, King had crossed Iowa into Illinois, stopping in Marshalltown, Chelsea and Cedar Rapids along the way to greet fans. King completed her journey forty-nine days after leaving Los Angeles and received a hero's welcome when she arrived in New York City on October 19, 1915.

Several ag commodity groups are headquartered in central Iowa, including the Iowa Turkey Federation, which is located at 535 East Lincoln Way in Ames. *Author's collection.*

Today, there are some time-honored spots along Lincoln Way in Ames that probably would have caught King's eye had they been around in 1915. There's the larger-than-life metal turkey outside the headquarters of the Iowa Turkey Federation at 535 East Lincoln Way. Just down the road is the Tip Top Lounge, complete with vintage neon signage.

The Tip Top has been located along Lincoln Way for more than seventy years. It opened as Bob's Tip Top Sandwich Shop in 1949. It was later purchased by Jim Overturg, who modified the name and transformed it into a lounge. It remains a popular hangout for Ames residents and visitors, whether you want a cold beer or a hot bowl of chili.

BURGERS TO BARBECUE ABOUND IN AMES

No matter what you're hungry for, Ames has long offered a range of food choices. Maybe it's a natural outgrowth of being a college town, since this is the home of Iowa State University (ISU).

If you love burgers, check out restaurants that have won the coveted Best Burger in Iowa Contest, including Brick City Grill (2640 Stange Road) and Café Beaudelaire (2504 Lincoln Way). I interviewed Claudio Gianello in May 2018 about what it was like for Café Beaudelaire to win this statewide honor from the Iowa Cattlemen's Association and Iowa Beef Industry Council (which happen to be located in Ames). He said customers from across Iowa and beyond filled every table in "Café B" in their quest to savor a beef masterpiece. "We were cooking 300 to 400 burgers a day after we won the award," said Brazilian-born Gianello, who serves up the soul of Brazil in the heart of Iowa, with a menu inspired by the street food of South America and Spain.

If American barbecue is more your style, head over to Hickory Park (1404 South Duff Avenue) for a taste of Ames history. The legend of Hickory Park started in May 1970. The restaurant quickly gained a reputation for excellent barbecue and ice cream for dessert—two traditions that have lived on as Hickory Park expanded twice. The current restaurant, which opened in 1997, can seat nearly 450 guests. "We serve over 20,000 pounds of meat to our average of 16,000 guests that dine with us each week," notes each Hickory Park menu. "With nearly 260 employees to serve you,

Fast food has long been part of America's car culture, and chain restaurants had become more common around the Lincoln Highway by the 1960s. John Dasher (shown here with his wife and Ronald McDonald) opened a new McDonald's restaurant on South Duff Avenue in Ames in February 1971. A 1971 *Ames Tribune* article noted that "McDonald's now boasts almost 1,700 restaurants in the country." By 2021, McDonald's operated and franchised 40,031 restaurants worldwide. Today, there's a McDonald's on Duff Avenue and one on Lincoln Way in Ames. *Courtesy of Ames History Museum.*

Hickory Park in Ames started in May 1970. The restaurant quickly gained a reputation for excellent barbecue and elaborate ice cream desserts. "We currently serve over 20,000 pounds of meat to our average of 16,000 guests that dine with us each week," notes Hickory Park's menu. *Author's collection.*

our humble goal remains the same, to earn our reputation with you each and every day!"

I've long been a fan of the Saucy Southerner, a perfect blend of smoked pork, turkey and beef simmered in barbecue sauce and served on your choice of white, wheat or onion bun (I always go for onion). With so much great food, it's tough to leave room for dessert, but really you must. Hickory Park serves an amazing array of ice cream treats crafted with Blue Bunny ice cream, which is made in Le Mars, Iowa, "the Ice Cream Capital of the World." With all the traditional sundaes and even candy bar sundaes like the Milky Way (vanilla ice cream, chocolate ice cream, caramel, whipped cream and a cherry on top), how can you go wrong? As one of my friends says, "How come ice cream desserts just taste better at Hickory Park?" I don't know, but they certainly do.

If you feel the need to burn off some calories, stop by Reiman Gardens in Ames. This seventeen-acre gem, which was created by a generous donation from Iowa native Roy Reiman and his wife, Bobbi, has graced the area south of ISU's campus since 1995. Reiman Gardens offers an ever-changing kaleidoscope of colors in the gardens. Hundreds of butterflies also enchant visitors in a tropical sanctuary known as the Christina Reiman Butterfly Wing. This year-round attraction never fails to convey beauty and showcase nature in a way that educates and inspires.

BOONE COUNTY

As you head to Boone County, it's clear that the history of this area has long been intertwined with the Lincoln Highway and the railroad. The James H. Andrew Railroad Museum in Boone (the county seat of Boone County) offers a wealth of information about the history of railroads in Iowa and America. Climb aboard and ride the Boone & Scenic Valley Railroad to enjoy some of the most beautiful scenery in the Midwest in the picturesque Des Moines River Valley.

One of the Boone area's most famous residents was Kate Shelley. On the night of July 6, 1881, a violent rainstorm hit near Honey Creek in the Des Moines River Valley. Fifteen-year-old Kate heard a locomotive tumble off the Honey Creek bridge into the water. As she carefully made her way across the broken parts of the bridge, the wind blew out her lantern. Undeterred, she pressed on to the depot in Moingona, Iowa, because she knew that the Midnight Limited was on its way.

Kate arrived in time for the agent to flag down the train and save many lives. A railroad bridge in the area was named in honor of Kate, who remained in Boone County and died at age forty-six in 1912.

As you're exploring local history, don't miss Ledges State Park near Boone. A four-mile trail system winds through steep slopes and scenic overviews, with sandstone ledges towering one hundred feet above the Des Moines River. Various 1930s Civilian Conservation Corps (CCC) structures can be viewed throughout the park, including a stone bridge.

Right: Boone County has a rich transportation history, from rail to road. On July 6, 1881, Kate Shelley, fifteen, heard a locomotive tumble off a nearby railroad bridge during a terrible nighttime storm. She risked her life navigating the broken bridge to reach the depot and warn of the danger. The young heroine saved many lives. *Courtesy of James H. Andrew Railroad Museum.*

Below: The Mamie Doud Eisenhower Birthplace at 709 Carroll Street in Boone (shown here in February 2021) honors Mamie Geneva Doud Eisenhower (1896–1979), wife of the thirty-fourth president, Dwight D. Eisenhower, and a popular first lady of the United States from 1953 to 1961. *Author's collection.*

Back in town, take a look at the Mamie Doud Eisenhower Birthplace at 709 Carroll Street in Boone. Mamie Geneva Doud Eisenhower (1896–1979) was the wife of the thirty-fourth president, Dwight D. Eisenhower, and a popular first lady of the United States from 1953 to 1961.

Mamie was born in Boone in 1896 and spent her early years in Cedar Rapids before her family moved to Colorado. At age nineteen, she married Dwight Eisenhower in 1916. (Here's a little Iowa trivia: Mamie was the second first lady to be born west of the Mississippi River. The first was Lou Henry Hoover, born in 1874 in Waterloo, Iowa.)

Mamie's Boone roots caught Iowans' attention as the U.S. Army convoy rolled across America in the summer of 1919. The *Boone News Republican* began printing stories about the convoy more than a week before the men made a brief stop in Boone. "I can't say too much on the condition of the Lincoln Highway," said Lieutenant Colonel Dwight Eisenhower, who visited relatives (the Carlsons) briefly while he was in town. During the hour in Boone, soldiers and local citizens mingled, and the Red Cross distributed ice cream to the dusty travelers.

Mamie, who was inducted into the Iowa Women's Hall of Fame in 1993, has another claim to fame, namely her Million-Dollar Fudge recipe. This used to be the go-to recipe for home cooks in the 1950s and 1960s. Million-Dollar Fudge was supposedly a favorite of Ike and Mamie, which might or might not be true. In any case, it's easy to make, and it's tasty.

Mamie Eisenhower's Million-Dollar Fudge

12 ounces semisweet chocolate morsels
12 ounces Baker's German's sweet chocolate, broken into small pieces
2 cups marshmallow cream
4½ cups sugar
Pinch salt
2 tablespoons butter
1½ cups (12 ounces) canned evaporated milk
2 cups coarsely chopped nuts (if desired)

Butter a 9-by-13-inch baking dish or mist it with nonstick cooking spray. Stir together the semisweet chocolate, German's chocolate and marshmallow cream in a large bowl. Bring the sugar, salt, butter and evaporated milk to a boil in a medium saucepan over medium-high heat. Boil for 1 minute. Reduce the heat and simmer 7 minutes, stirring continuously. Pour the hot syrup over the chocolate mixture and stir until smooth. Stir in the nuts, if desired. Pour fudge into the prepared pan. Let stand undisturbed at room temperature until firm, preferably overnight. Cut the fudge into small squares. Store in an airtight container for up to 2 weeks.

THE SEARCH FOR IOWA'S BEST TENDERLOIN

As you head west from Boone, there are plenty of interesting attractions along four-lane Highway 30. Thousands of people fill the grandstands throughout the summer at the Boone Speedway for dirt track racing, from World of Outlaws competitions to the IMCA Speedway Motors Super Nationals and more.

Seven Oaks Recreation just west of Boone offers year-round fun, including paintball, canoeing, kayaking, tube floating, camping, snow skiing, snowboarding and snow tubing. If agriculture is more your style, the Farm

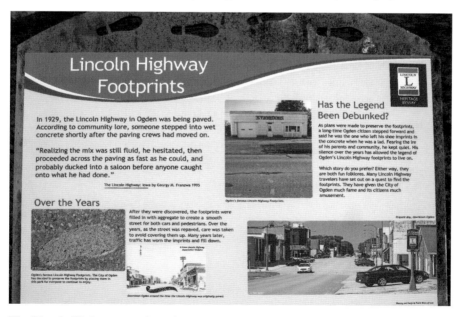

The Lincoln Highway runs through downtown Ogden. After crews paved this road in 1929, someone walked across the highway before the pavement had dried, leaving footprints forever in the road. The footprints were patched up, although they were still visible for years, as this sign in Ogden notes. *Author's collection.*

Progress Show is held every other August at the Central Iowa Expo Center near the intersection of Highway 30 and 17. The nation's largest outdoor farm event hosts more than six hundred exhibitors and attracts hundreds of thousands of farmers and agribusiness professionals from forty-six states and around the world.

Food and farming are a natural fit in Iowa, especially when it comes to pork. Iowans know good pork, whether it's a thick, juicy Iowa chop or a huge-as-a-dinner-plate breaded pork tenderloin sandwich like you'll find in Ogden, another Lincoln Highway town in Boone County.

The Lucky Pig Pub & Grill in Ogden earned Iowa's Best Tenderloin honors in October 2014, just in time for October Pork Month. Since 2003, the Iowa Pork Producers Association (IPPA) has hosted the Iowa's Best Tenderloin contest, and the competition seems to get tougher each year. (When the Lucky Pig won top honors, the IPPA received more than 1,900 nominations from tenderloin fanatics.)

The prestigious award helped the Lucky Pig attract customers from almost every Iowa county and every state surrounding Iowa. The restaurant sold about six hundred tenderloins in just one day following the big announcement. If you're in Boone County, stop by the Lucky Pig and try a tenderloin. If you'd like to try making your own, here's a recipe from my friend Cristen Clark, a sixth-generation farmer, wife, mother, blogger and award-winning cook/baker from Runnells, Iowa.

Classic Iowa Pork Tenderloin Sandwich

1 cup all-purpose flour
1 cup cornstarch
2 teaspoons seasoned salt
1 teaspoon ground black pepper
2 eggs
3 tablespoons milk
1 sleeve Chicken in a Biskit crackers, crushed
1 cup panko bread crumbs
4 boneless pork loin chops
1 quart peanut or vegetable oil
4 large sandwich or Kaiser rolls, split and buttered
Dill pickles, ketchup, mustard, thinly sliced sweet onions

Combine the flour, cornstarch, seasoned salt and pepper in a shallow baking dish. Remove and reserve 2 tablespoons of this mixture. In a second shallow baking dish, whisk the eggs and milk together until well blended. In a third dish, combine the crushed crackers and panko, plus the reserved flour/cornstarch mixture.

Butterfly each pork chop and pound between sheets of plastic wrap with a meat mallet to ¼-inch thick.

To coat, first dredge each piece of pork on both sides in seasoned flour, shaking off any excess. Dip into the egg mixture to coat both sides, then dredge in the crumb mixture, pressing gently to coat both sides evenly. Transfer the pork to a clean plate and repeat the process with the remaining pork. Allow the pork to rest for 20 minutes to give the breading time to adhere to the meat.

In a large, heavy-bottomed skillet, heat the oil to 350°F. Fry the breaded pork until golden brown on both sides, about 3 minutes per side. The pork is cooked when it reaches an internal temperature of 145°F on an instant-read thermometer. Transfer to paper towel–lined plate.

DON'T MISS BOONE COUNTY'S RAINBOW BRIDGE

As you head west, do a little "gravel travel" north of the tiny town of Beaver to see a rare "rainbow bridge" spanning Beaver Creek along the old Lincoln Highway. This concrete bridge was built by the Des Moines–based N.E. Marsh & Son Construction Company, using a design from James Marsh, an Iowa State graduate, engineer and patent holder for the rainbow arch configuration.

When this bridge was built in 1919, it allowed the Lincoln Highway to be routed west out of Ogden north of the railroad, eliminating several dangerous railroad crossings. The Lincoln Highway remained on this route until the 1920s, when it was again moved south, noted the booklet "Marsh Rainbow Arch Bridges in Iowa," which is available at publications.iowa.gov.

The aesthetic appeal of the rainbow arch was always a selling point. "Marsh's design allowed even rural townships to have bridges that… matched the elegant style of the times that adorned the river crossings in the big cities," the booklet noted.

This distinctive rainbow-arch bridge, which is still standing, was built in 1919 over the creek north of Beaver. This allowed the Lincoln Highway to be routed west out of Ogden north of the railroad, eliminating several dangerous railroad crossings. *Author's collection.*

While there were at least a few hundred Marsh rainbow arch bridges built around the Midwest in the early twentieth century, many are gone. At the time the "Marsh Rainbow" booklet was published in 1997, it noted that only nine of these bridges remained in Iowa. The Beaver Creek Rainbow Arch Bridge endures today and is still in use.

GREENE COUNTY

As you head into Greene County, you're entering the heart of some of Iowa's most exceptional Lincoln Highway history. Besides the "seedling mile" in Linn County, Greene County was the first county in Iowa to pave its portion of the Lincoln Highway.

Greene County also became one of the first counties in Iowa to develop drainage districts—an important consideration in this part of the state, where excess water needed to be redirected from the landscape, not only to help crops thrive in the rich, black soil, but also to allow durable roads to be built. By the early 1900s, Greene County was investing in drainage systems, improved roads and modern bridges, including the Eureka Bridge over the Raccoon River. In fact, the preservation of this bridge became the flashpoint that revitalized the Lincoln Highway Association (LHA) in the early 1990s.

Constructed in 1913, the five-arch Eureka Bridge over the North Raccoon River had been widened in 1924 for Lincoln Highway traffic. By 1991, however, there were plans to bypass it in favor of a new road. "Around this time, a state law was passed that road construction should consider historic preservation," said Bob Ausberger, a Jefferson-area farmer and longtime Lincoln Highway fan. "That was really a big victory."

Ausberger and his wife, Joyce, who are now in their early eighties, are still enthusiastic about preserving the heritage connected with the Lincoln Highway. "We have something here that's really unique," Joyce said.

The fight to save Eureka Bridge prompted the Ausbergers to help form the Greene County Lincoln Highway Association. This sparked the rebirth

Jefferson-area residents Bob and Joyce Ausberger (shown here in 2021) volunteer at Iowa's Lincoln Highway Museum in downtown Grand Junction. The Ausbergers, who farm in Greene County, are passionate about historic preservation and helped form the modern national Lincoln Highway Association in 1992. *Author's collection.*

of the LHA in 1992. The couple has been "working on Lincoln Highway stuff" for half of their sixty-one-year marriage, Joyce noted. "There's always some little thing that will spur us on," she added.

You might just meet the Ausbergers if you stop by the Lincoln Highway Museum, which is housed in a former bank in downtown Grand Junction. This little museum is packed with vintage Lincoln Highway signs, old photographs and other treasures. Nearby is the Grand Junction Lincoln Highway Garden, which is designed in the shape of United States with the "Lincoln Highway" path running through it.

While you're in Grand Junction, head over to Lions Club Tree Park east of town. You can drive through this Lincoln Highway interpretation area, where signage tells the story of the Lincoln Highway.

If you take the old Lincoln Highway out of Grand Junction, you can see traces of the past, from a former gas station to the old Star Motel on the south edge of town. Once you reach Jefferson, you'll discover Lincoln Highway heritage everywhere along Lincoln Way. Don't miss the Freedom Rock by the old Milligan grain elevator near the restored Milwaukee Railroad Depot, which serves as the trail head for the Raccoon River Valley

Greene County's Freedom Rock by the old Milligan grain elevator is near the restored Milwaukee Railroad Depot, which serves as the trail head for the Raccoon River Valley Trail. The painted boulder shows four patriotic scenes of local history, including Dwight Eisenhower and the 1919 U.S. Army motor transport convoy traveling across the Lincoln Highway. *Author's collection.*

Trail. Ray "Bubba" Sorensen, an artist from Greenfield, Iowa, and member of the Iowa House of Representatives, painted the Freedom Rock in 2016. (In fact, Sorensen has painted a Freedom Rock in each of Iowa's ninety-nine counties to honor veterans.) The Freedom Rock in Jefferson shows four patriotic scenes of local history, including the 1919 U.S. Army motor transport convoy traveling the Lincoln Highway.

Keep heading west and you'll come to the Greene County Historical Society, where you can explore Lincoln Highway history and more. Go another block and you're at the town square, where the current Greene County Courthouse has stood since 1917. The Abraham Lincoln statue on the south side of the courthouse square was erected in 1918. It was a gift from local resident E.B. Wilson to commemorate the Lincoln Highway, which passed directly in front of the monument.

Lincoln stands near the Mahanay Memorial Carillon Tower. The 168-foot-tall carillon tower was given to the people of Jefferson and Greene County in accordance with the wills of Mr. and Mrs. Floyd Mahanay. The tower was dedicated in October 1966, complete with fourteen bells cast at the world-famous Petit & Fritsen bell foundry in Holland. Since then, more bells have been added, and they chime daily.

Attention chocolate lovers! A luscious layer cake called Better than Bell Tower Cake is a signature dessert at The Centennial (100 East State Street), a new dining experience where contemporary taste meets historic charm in a beautifully renovated 146-year-old building on the Bell Tower Square.

In 1980, volunteers organized the first Bell Tower Festival, inspired by the Mahanay Memorial Carillon Tower. You can ride to the top of the tower via an elevator and view the horizon from the glass-enclosed Paul Nally Observation Deck. You may even notice some artwork in surprising places—on the rooftops of downtown Jefferson.

Six unique pieces of rooftop art have been installed since 2015, including *Wild Woman on the Roof*, created by local artist Nicole Friess-Schilling. Then there's *Spaceman*, which honors Greene County native son Loren Shriver, an astronaut who grew up in Paton. *Patches of Greene*, which includes four quilt squares painted on sheets of aluminum,

Built in 1923, this former Deep Rock service station is located along the Lincoln Highway in Jefferson. It was best known as "Pete and Paul's" (since Paul McNulty and Pete Garrity ran it from 1951 to 1976). When a customer pulled in, a bell attached to the rubber hose on the station's driveway would ring. An attendant would pump the gas, wash the vehicle's windshield, check the tires and ask, "What else can we do for you?" *Author's collection.*

This Abraham Lincoln statue at the courthouse square in Jefferson was erected in 1918 to commemorate the nearby Lincoln Highway. Lincoln stands near the Mahanay Memorial Carillon Tower, which was dedicated in October 1966. You can ride to the top of the tower and scan the horizon from the glass-enclosed observation deck, plus the carillon chimes throughout the day. *Author's collection.*

Right: From the Mahanay Bell Tower, you can see art on the rooftops of downtown Jefferson. They include "Patches of Greene," shown here. The four quilt squares painted on sheets of aluminum represent important aspects of Greene County, from railroad history to wind energy. *Author's collection.*

Below: This distinctive octagonal house at 703 South Chestnut Street in Jefferson was built in 1902. This was the boyhood home of Dr. George Gallup, the father of public opinion polling. The renovated home (shown here in 2017) is in the National Register of Historic Places. *Author's collection.*

represents important aspects of Greene County, from the railroad to wind energy.

As you take in the view, you might be able to spot a distinctive octagonal house a few blocks to the south of the town square. Located at 703 South Chestnut Street, this was the boyhood home of George Gallup, the father of public-opinion polling. Built in 1902, this renovated home is in the National Register of Historic Places.

When you're back on the ground, discover more art in the pocket park south of the courthouse square, enjoy an ice cream treat (and a cool painted mural) at the Twins Shoppe nearby on Lincoln Way or head over to the Thomas Jefferson Gardens of Greene County, Iowa (TJGGCI), southeast of the courthouse square. These gardens honor the legacy and ideals of President Thomas Jefferson, who frequently extolled the virtues of the agrarian life and championed self-government.

A great deal of work went into creating the nearly $1 million gardens that visitors enjoy today. After extensive grant writing and fundraising, volunteers added the first plants to the garden in 2014. Brick paving connects the five distinct gardens in the TJGGCI, including the farmer's

The Thomas Jefferson Gardens of Greene County, Iowa (TJGGCI), in downtown Jefferson, honor President Thomas Jefferson, who extolled the virtues of the agrarian life and self-government. The gardens include native plants, outdoor musical instruments, Buck roses (hardy varieties developed by Dr. Griffith Buck from Iowa State University) and more. *Author's collection.*

Located west of Jefferson, Deal's Orchard is a fourth-generation business (owner Jerald Deal is shown here) whose roots date to 1917. An agri-tourism destination, Deal's Orchard is known for its high-quality apples, cider, hard cider, gift items, family fun zone and more. *Author's collection.*

There are many Iowa Century Farms (owned by the same family for 100 years or more) and Heritage Farms (owned by the same family for 150 years or more) near the Lincoln Highway. The Clark family's Heritage Farm (which dates to 1856) is in Junction Township, and their Century Farm (which dates to 1894) is in Jackson Township in Greene County. *Author's collection.*

garden (which includes a replica of a plow that Jefferson designed), a prairie garden filled with native plants, a children's garden, a flower and rose garden including Buck roses (hardy varieties developed by Dr. Griffith Buck from Iowa State University) and raised-bed gardens.

Since Thomas Jefferson was interested in music as well as agriculture, the gardens also include whimsical, larger-than-life musical instruments, including a contra base chime and xylophone you can play. Volunteers continue to look for ways to improve the garden. "A garden is always a work in progress," said Jean Walker, a TJGGCI volunteer.

Explore more horticultural heritage west of Jefferson near the Lincoln Highway at Deal's Orchard. The fourth generation of the Deal family runs this orchard and agri-tourism destination, whose roots date back to 1917. Enjoy Deal's Orchard apples, cider and hard cider, holiday gift baskets and more in the Apple Barn. In the fall, explore the family fun zone and Apple Acres, which includes a corn pool, pedal tractors and more.

Your next stop is Scranton, which is home to the oldest working water tower in Iowa and the ninth oldest in the nation, according to Lincoln Highway signage. The "Our History" section of www.scrantoniowa.com adds that the water tower, built in 1897, was the first steel elevated water tank built by Pittsburgh–Des Moines Steel.

Moss Markers Honor Abraham Lincoln

As you head north from Scranton, cross Highway 30 and go west around the curve of the old Lincoln Highway, you'll notice two striking white monuments. These are the famed Moss markers, and they have quite an illustrious history.

Their story begins with James E. Moss during the Civil War. The seventeen-year-old from Illinois enlisted in the Fox River Regiment of the Illinois Thirty-Sixth Volunteers, which later became part of the Union's Army of the Cumberland, according to a 2001 article in the *Carroll Times Herald* about the Moss markers.

Moss suffered serious injuries during the battle of Missionary Ridge near Chattanooga, Tennessee, in 1863. Part of his left leg had to be amputated a few days later. President Abraham Lincoln personally decorated Moss for his service and bravery. "He lived with a peg leg for the rest of his life," noted Jonathan Fletcher (1914–2004) of Des Moines, Moss's grandson, who spoke at a ceremony at the Moss markers in 2001. "Moss was a staunch supporter

Union army veteran James E. Moss (*second from right*) lost part of his left leg following a Civil War battle in 1863. Abraham Lincoln decorated Moss for his bravery. To honor the former president, Moss installed monuments featuring busts of Lincoln at both ends of the curve around his farmland on the Lincoln Highway north of Scranton. *Courtesy of University of Michigan Library.*

of the Union, thought the Civil War was justified, and all of his life he was a great admirer of Abraham Lincoln."

Moss moved to Iowa in 1875 and became a successful pioneer farmer. He acquired a number of farms in the Scranton area due, in part, to land warrants, noted Kirk Citurs, who farms some of this Greene County land in Kendrick Township.

In the early to mid-1800s, the federal government sometimes paid military veterans with land warrants—certificates that could be redeemed for U.S. public land. Some of Moss's friends from Illinois had warrants for land in west-central Iowa but had no desire to move west. They sold Moss the land instead. "He ended up with 3 sections [1,920 acres of land]," Citurs said. "Moss and his wife had six daughters, and the daughters each got a half section of land." Citurs's family has farmed one of those half sections since 1969. This parcel was the last of the Moss land to be sold out of the Moss family when it changed hands in 2018, Citurs added.

During his lifetime, Moss's farming enterprises made him a wealthy man. He raised horses and sold them through the Sears Roebuck & Company catalogue, Citurs said. Moss's name was also noted in the *National Register of French Draft Horses* book, published in 1884. As his profits grew, Moss used some of his money to donate a church organ to the Methodist church in Scranton. He also built a large home in Scranton.

As motorized horsepower began to replace traditional horsepower and the Lincoln Highway took shape, Moss was appointed a Lincoln Highway consul to help promote the highway in the local area. When Greene County prepared to pave the Lincoln Highway in 1924 in Moss's area, Moss thought that modern, faster cars should travel on rounded corners, rather than square corners. To widen the curve on a section of the Lincoln Highway north of Scranton, the county needed about half an acre of farmland that Moss owned.

J.L. Lindsey, who was the Greene County engineer at the time, shared his memories of this project. "We went to see Mr. Moss and asked him to sell us the land. He said he would give it to us if we arranged to install busts of Lincoln at either end of the curve," said Lindsey in an undated, unnamed newspaper clipping displayed in the Greene County Historical Society in Jefferson.

Moss told Lindsey that he wanted the busts as a tribute to his former commander-in-chief and that he would pay for them himself, according to the article "They Still Stand: Trades Half Acre for Right to Put Up Busts of Lincoln." Lindsey reached out to Harold "Tom" Carlisle, a Jefferson, Iowa native who was a student at the University of Iowa at the time. Known for his artistic talent, Carlisle would succeed the famed J.N. "Ding" Darling as a *Des Moines Register* cartoonist after Darling retired. "Carlisle carved the head [of Lincoln] and then made a form of it out of papier mâché, which he sent to us," Lindsey said. "The busts that stand at either end of the curve were made by pouring concrete inside the form."

The two Moss markers were installed near the section of the Lincoln Highway north of Scranton that became the first fifty-mile-per-hour curve in Greene County. The idea for curved corners in the highway caught on, and other counties followed suit. The markers were a point of pride for Moss, who died in 1932 at age eighty-nine and was buried at the Scranton Cemetery.

"Except for the unavoidable erosion of time, the busts today stand unharmed, and that, says Lindsey, is a remarkable and inspiring thing," noted the undated newspaper article. "'Through the years, people have shot holes into signs and posts all over the county, but nobody has ever wanted to mutilate the busts of Lincoln,' Lindsey concluded."

That changed around 1968, when vandals broke off the bust of Lincoln atop the east monument, Citurs said. They left the hatchet or axe at the scene of the crime by the north monument. For years, the Moss markers looked more like tombstones, after the busts of Lincoln were gone.

Then, something mysterious happened in the 1990s. A woman contacted a district court judge in northern Iowa who was originally from Jefferson. She told him that she had something she wanted him to have, and it was in a metal filing box. She laid out some specific conditions though. "I've got the original head," meaning the long-gone bust of Abe Lincoln, but "don't ask me any details."

The bust was returned to Greene County during the annual Bell Tower Festival in Jefferson. Area residents worked to restore the Moss monuments. Local Lincoln Highway supporters helped organize a ceremony on August 27, 2001, for the unveiling of the restored Lincoln busts. About fifty people, including J.E. Moss's last living grandchildren and Jonathan Fletcher and his first cousin, Susan Thomas Feldner, gathered with other Moss family descendants and Lincoln Highway enthusiasts for the event at the "Moss corner."

While vandals damaged the Moss markers at various times through the years and even stole the busts of Lincoln, the monuments (shown here in 2014) have been restored and continue to greet travelers on the old Lincoln Highway in Greene County. *Author's collection.*

During the ceremony by the soybean field, Fletcher pulled a purple velvet cloth off the restored bust of Lincoln, stood eye to eye with Honest Abe and smiled. "I was really thrilled," Fletcher told the *Carroll Times Herald*. He also shared his memories of crews paving the Lincoln Highway near Scranton in 1924, when he was visiting his cousin Susan and her family. "It was a great occasion."

Unfortunately, vandals didn't leave the Moss markers alone. Around 2010, they stole the bust off the north marker. "I noticed it immediately," said Citurs, who added that more vandalism occurred at the markers around the winter solstice.

While the papier mâché molds that had been used to make the original busts of Lincoln had been stored in the Greene County Courthouse for years, they were long gone. Locals turned to Dennis Meyer of Created in Johnston, who makes concrete statues, to help with the restoration process. "Now we have the mold, so we can make more," Citurs said.

Since he farms in the area, Citurs takes a special interest in the Moss markers. He paints the bases as needed and uses a string trimmer to remove weeds. He likes to keep the markers looking nice, since people sometimes stop by to take pictures. "The Moss markers are unique, artistic creations that offer a stunning likeness of Abe Lincoln," Citurs said.

CARROLL COUNTY

As you leave Greene County and head to Carroll County, check out the tiny town of Ralston, which is helping power the future. REG Ralston is a biodiesel plant that makes fuel from soy oil processed from locally grown soybeans. This fuel powers semitrucks and more. "The world is demanding sustainability solutions," said Bill Ritchie, plant manager of REG Ralston, when I interviewed him in 2019. "Our biodiesel is part of the answer, plus it adds value to Iowa's soybean crop and the state's rural communities."

As you head west to Glidden, watch for the plastic ice cream cones in front of the Dairy Mart. If you see a yellow ice cream cone, you're in luck. It's lemon ice cream time, and that's definitely worth a trip through the drive-thru, where you can also get burgers, tenderloins and more.

Just down the road, there was a time when you could have enjoyed an exceptional dinner at Mr. D's, a popular restaurant that was part of Glidden for decades. Newspaper advertisements from the 1970s show that Mr. D's, which Denny and Karen Heuton operated for many years, featured live music along with great food. Today, Mr. D's is the Lincoln Club, an event venue.

East of town, watch for the large granite marker at the Merle Hay Memorial Cemetery, which connects to a recreational trail. This marker pays tribute to Private Merle D. Hay, a Glidden native and one of the first American soldiers killed in World War I. Hay enlisted in the U.S. Army in May 1917. On November 3, 1917, the twenty-one-year-old soldier was killed in combat near Artois, France.

D's Mister

Glidden, Iowa

Greeting You Nightly
KAREN & DENNY HEUTON

FRI. and SAT.
MARCH 29-30
SLOE—MOTION

Tuesday thru Saturday
April 2-6
JANE RUSSELL TRIO

OPEN SUNDAYS - 12 noon to 8 p.m.
CLOSED MONDAYS

Above: A plastic yellow ice cream cone in front of the Dairy Mart in Glidden means it's lemon ice cream time. You can also get breaded pork tenderloin sandwiches, burgers and other menu items. Some items are named in honor of the Wildcats, the mascot of Glidden-Ralston schools. *Author's collection.*

Left: Mr. D's, a popular restaurant in Glidden for years, featured live music, along with great meals, back in the day, as evidenced by this newspaper ad that appeared in the *Lake City Graphic* in 1974. *Courtesy of Central School Preservation, Lake City.*

A large granite marker at the Merle Hay Memorial Cemetery pays tribute to Private Merle D. Hay, a Glidden native and one of the first American soldiers killed in World War I. He was killed in combat in France on November 3, 1917. *Author's collection.*

When the 1919 army convoy came through Glidden on its cross-country trip on the Lincoln Highway, it made a special stop to pay respects to the fallen soldier. Hay's body was later returned home to Glidden, where he is buried at the local cemetery. An estimated ten to twenty thousand people attended his memorial service on July 24, 1921—an amazing number of people for a town of nine hundred residents, noted the Lincoln Highway Association.

On May 25, 1930, an estimated six thousand people gathered at the cemetery for the dedication of a large granite monument featuring an image of Uncle Sam carrying the lifeless body of a young soldier. The haunting artwork—created by Jay "Ding" Darling, a Pulitzer Prize–winning cartoonist and noted Iowa conservationist—is flanked by an inscription "to commemorate the sacrifice of Merle D. Hay and all his Iowa comrades who gave their lives for our country during the World War."

As you continue your journey west and arrive in Carroll, look for various historic buildings along the Lincoln Highway, including the former Carnegie library, which was dedicated in 1905 and now houses the Carroll County Historical Museum. Effie Gladding and her husband likely saw this building when they came through Carroll in 1914. The well-to-do Gladdings were concluding a 'round-the-world trip with an auto tour that summer from San Francisco to their home in Montclair, New Jersey.

After several weeks among the "uncivilized westerners," the Gladdings arrived late one day in Carroll. "As we approached Carroll, we came to a hill top from which we looked down on a valley of tasseled corn fields," Effie Gladding wrote. "It was exactly like looking down on an immense, shining green rug, with yellow tufts thrown up over its green surface. We saw but few orchards. This was a corn country. We were surprised to find so good a hotel as Burke's Hotel in a small town."

She was somewhat shocked, however, by the locals. "We were obliged to take our supper at a restaurant near the hotel. We were interested in four young people who were evidently out for a good time. The two young gentlemen, by a liberal use of 25-cent pieces, kept the mechanical piano pounding out music all through their meal. They were both guiltless of coats and waist-coats. We had seen all through the West men in all sorts of public assemblies, more or less formal, wearing only their shirts and trousers. So, we had become somewhat accustomed to what we called the shirt-waist habit."

The Gladdings may have wanted some wine after that "distressing" experience, but Carroll's locally produced wine options were decades in the future. In recent years, wine has defined the historic building along the Lincoln Highway that once housed the Wittrock auto dealership, especially since John and Rose Guinan converted it into Santa Maria Winery around 2008. Today, a number of local shops carry a variety of Santa Maria wines, including Lincoln Highway, a blend of cherry, raspberry and wild plum flavors, with a smooth finish.

Farther to the west, you'll see Carroll's historic train depot, which was built in 1896. In the 1990s, the community restored the depot, which is now home to the Carroll Chamber of Commerce. Visitors are invited to stop and watch the trains go by.

If you'd like to take home a memento of your trip to Carroll, there are many shopping

The Santa Maria Winery has been part of Carroll County since 2008 and produces a variety of wines, including Lincoln Highway, known for its refreshing cherry, raspberry and wild plum flavors, with a pleasantly smooth finish. *Author's collection.*

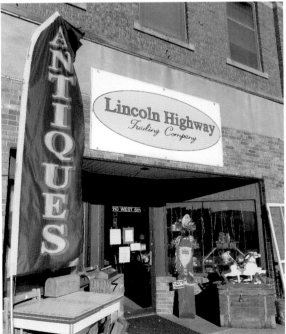

Above: Carroll's historic train depot, which was built in 1896, was restored in the 1990s and houses the Carroll Chamber of Commerce. This crowd gathered there on July 15, 2019, to see the Union Pacific's "Big Boy" 4014 steam engine on its Midwest tour. *Author's collection.*

Left: Carroll is a shopping destination with something for every budget, thanks to an array of thrift shops and antique stores, including the Lincoln Highway Trading Company downtown. *Author's collection.*

By the 1930s and 1940s, semipro baseball had begun to thrive in Carroll. Since 1949, teams have played at Merchants Park Stadium, which has also hosted the state high school baseball tournament in recent years. *Author's collection.*

destinations, especially if you like second-hand treasures. There are a wealth of thrift shops and antique stores here, including the Lincoln Highway Trading Company downtown.

Before you leave town, take in a Carroll Merchants baseball game if you can. Carroll maintains a baseball tradition dating back to the 1870s. By the 1930s and 1940s, semipro baseball was thriving in Carroll. By 1948, plans (and fundraising) were underway for a modern, 1,500-seat Merchants Park Stadium. On June 10, 1949, Merchants Park Stadium officially opened with a game between the Carroll Merchants and the Harlan Cardinals (who won 6–0) before 3,233 fans.

Teams continue to play baseball games at Merchants Park. In 2021, state high school baseball tournament games were also held at Merchants Park, and more are planned for 2022.

CHURCH TURNED HOME DATES TO 1879

As you head west on the Lincoln Highway toward Arcadia, imagine, if you will, a church rolling down the road. It was quite a sight, that September day in 2012 when an old wooden church rolled east along Highway 30.

"It was scary to watch, even though the crew did a great job," said Laurie Blum, who transformed this 1879 church into a farm home with the help of her husband, Joe.

Located about a mile east of Arcadia, the repurposed church graces the Blum's acreage, accented by mature trees and a large pond. "People often pull off the highway here to take pictures," Joe said.

The Presbyterian church had been located in Arcadia for more than 125 years. The congregation, which had dwindled to just a handful of members, held its last service on November 13, 2005. "I started thinking about all the joy in this church through the years," Laurie said. "I felt a heart touch to turn the church into a home."

The Blums bought the twenty-four-by-forty-foot church for $30,000 in 2010. When they were ready to move it in September 2012, the trip involved crossing the busy railroad tracks on the south edge of town and passing safely along Highway 30, with help from Carroll County sheriff's deputies and the Iowa State Patrol. The church's tall spire meant that power lines had to be taken down temporarily, shutting off power to Arcadia.

After Joe and Laurie Blum bought the former Presbyterian church in Arcadia in 2010, they moved it to their acreage east of Arcadia in 2012. The church is now an integral part of the Blums' beautiful home and offers a unique view of historic preservation in rural Iowa. *Author's collection.*

Today, the church's original pine doors open into an entryway at the Blums' home. The former sanctuary, which has seventeen-foot-high ceilings with a center peak of twenty-three feet, houses the living room. The former altar area includes a kitchen where the church's original Bible rests on a pulpit incorporated into the cabinetry. The church also includes additions to accommodate bedrooms, porches and more. "This church is a treasure," Laurie. "My hope is that people will see it and say a little prayer."

FAC REMAINS A FARMER-OWNED CO-OP

As you drive west to Arcadia (which was originally called "Tip Top"), check out the signage explaining the Mississippi-Missouri Divide (elevation 1,429 feet). All water east of this point flows to the Mississippi River, while all water west flows to the Missouri River.

As you reach Arcadia, you'll notice the big white grain elevator to the north. That's FAC, a farmer-owned cooperative that has served the area for decades. When Darrell Henkenius was named CEO of the farmer-owned FAC on March 1, 2021, he became the fourth general manager in the cooperative's history. "A lot has changed since I started working with the co-op forty-plus years ago, but farmers still need places like FAC."

FAC in Arcadia is a farmer-owned cooperative that has served local producers since 1937. FAC allows farmers to work together for their mutual benefit, buying inputs to grow their crops, marketing their grain (shown here at the main office in 2015) and purchasing feed for their livestock. *Author's collection.*

This roadside marker along Highway 30 east of Arcadia notes the Mississippi-Missouri Divide (elevation 1,429 feet), where all water east of this point flows to the Mississippi River, while all water west flows to the Missouri River. *Author's collection.*

FAC became a farmer-owned cooperative in 1937. FAC helps farmers to work together to buy inputs for their crops, market their grain and purchase livestock feed. FAC also includes a lumberyard where FAC members and other customers can purchase supplies for home improvement projects. "You've got to know your customers," Henkenius said. "Listen to your members, so you can better serve their needs."

Arcadia Meats Is a Cut Above

Agriculture is reflected along the Lincoln Highway in many businesses, including Arcadia Meats. People gained a whole new appreciation for small-town Iowa businesses like this in 2020, when COVID-19 pandemic lockdowns spurred some panic buying, which led to some empty grocery shelves. "People suddenly didn't have access to all the items they wanted," said Dan Julin, owner/operator of Arcadia Meats. "More people started paying attention to the fact that meat doesn't come from the grocery store."

This created new opportunities for Arcadia Meats, which offers products to fit a range of budgets, from steaks to ground beef to Irv's Beef Jerky. "Before my Grandpa Irv passed away in 1996, he worked with my dad, Steve, to create Irv's Jerky and many other products our customers like," Julin said. "Grandpa Irv lives on every time someone buys some of his famous jerky."

Arcadia Meats is known for providing high-quality, locally produced food for decades. Housed in a meat locker that was built in 1950, the business first came into the Julin family when Grandpa Irv and his son Steve purchased Arcadia Meats in 1976.

Today, Arcadia Meats includes custom processing services for beef, pork, lamb, deer and other meats. For more than fifteen years, Arcadia Meats has been a wholesale distributor, serving customers in a radius of 90 to 120 miles around Arcadia. The business also includes a retail store in downtown Arcadia. Vintage and current photographs on the walls around the coolers in the retail store create a mini-museum showcasing the history of Arcadia and the meat locker, which has expanded multiple times in the past thirty years.

"For us, it's not just about having a job or business," notes the Arcadia Meats website. "It's about life lessons, passion, tradition, generations to come, family (immediate, employees, customers and you), and the smile that comes with the last bite."

Dan Julin and his family own and operate Arcadia Meats, a meat processing plant in Arcadia where customers can buy an array of beef and pork products. Popular items include Irv's Beef Jerky, which Dan's grandfather developed years ago. *Author's collection.*

The Julin family's contributions haven't gone unnoticed. In the spring of 2021, Arcadia Meats received the Outstanding Service Award during the Crawford County Cattlemen's banquet. As Arcadia Meats continues to evolve, the company's website summarizes the Julin family's philosophy best: "Wishing you a wonderful life and a full stomach."

DANCE AT THE ARCADIA LEGION HALL

If you're in downtown Arcadia, also check out the Arcadia Legion Hall, which includes western Iowa's largest, oldest dance hall. It dates back to the 1940s, an era when many small towns and cities throughout Iowa and beyond boasted a ballroom.

After Arcadia's verein hall (a social center for the local German American community) burned in 1944, residents wanted to build another community center. The building you see today was constructed in 1948 on land purchased for one dollar from the Duetscher Verein, a local organization formed to promote German culture.

As the community pledged money to build the new community hall, the total reached $30,000. When the cost of the project came in closer to $45,000 (more than $500,000 in 2022 dollars), project leaders asked for more donations, rather than taking out a loan. Generous supporters donated another $15,000 to get the job done.

Many local members of American Legion Post 694 and other citizens helped construct the seventy-one-by-one-hundred-foot building. The building contains a unique structure known as a lamella roof. Also known as the "Zollinger roof" (after Friedrich Zollinger, a German engineer), this vaulted ceiling is made from a crisscrossing pattern of parallel arches that span large spaces. The individual pieces are joined together with bolts and/or plates to form a rhomboid/diamond-shaped pattern. The lamella roof design became popular between the world wars.

Arcadia's new ballroom was designed so that the main floor could function not only as a dance floor but also an auditorium and gymnasium, with a stage at one end. The basement included a kitchen, coat check rooms,

The Arcadia Legion Hall includes western Iowa's largest and oldest dance hall (shown here in 2017). After the local verein hall (a social center for the German American community) burned in 1944, the community constructed this new building in 1948, where famous bands and artists from Lawrence Welk to Les Brown performed. *Author's collection.*

dressing rooms and other space. People throughout the region gathered at the new ballroom on July 5, 1949, to enjoy a free dance that was hosted to thank everyone who donated to the new building.

Through the years, many popular bands and artists played at the Arcadia Legion Hall, including Lawrence Welk, Les Brown, Guy Lombardo, Sammy Kay and many more. In those days, the admission price was seventy-five cents, including tax, with modern dance on Tuesday nights and old-time dances on Thursdays. The all-time biggest attendance at an Arcadia Legion Hall dance occurred on December 28, 1951, when 2,018 people gathered to hear Lawrence Welk perform.

Even if you couldn't be there in person, live radio broadcasts brought the activities from the ballroom into local residents' homes for years. KCIM Radio from Carroll broadcast a half-hour show every weekend, according to a history of the building displayed in the basement.

I took it all in when I stopped by the ballroom with my parents on the afternoon of Sunday, July 2, 2017. We came to watch people dance to the music of the Malek's Fishermen Band, one of the Midwest's finest polka bands. As I watched the dancers, I could almost imagine couples from years past gliding across the wooden floor, whether they came to waltz, foxtrot, polka or square dance (which was popular on Sunday evenings). Today, when people gather to celebrate a wedding or anniversary, the Arcadia Legion Hall remains a place where memories are made.

CRAWFORD COUNTY

If you like wide-open spaces, you'll appreciate Crawford County. Abraham Lincoln once owned land in Crawford County, although he never set foot in Goodrich Township. Lincoln received this land from the U.S. government for his service in the Black Hawk War of 1832. The land passed out of the Lincoln family many years ago, but a historical marker on a boulder still denotes where Lincoln's former land is located, north of Denison.

As you enter Crawford County from the east along the Lincoln Highway, you'll go through Westside, where you can visit the Eugene Kock Memorial Park. Dedicated to a local serviceman who was killed in action in Vietnam, the park also honors all service men and women who have served America. Down the road, you'll also see local history reflected in a restored gas station in Vail, which calls itself a "small town with a big heart."

Soon you'll arrive in Denison, the county seat of Crawford County. Look for Donna Reed Drive, which is named in honor of the Hollywood star who never forgot her Crawford County roots. She was born Donna Belle Mullenger in 1921 and grew up on a farm south of Denison. (While the farmhouse is gone, you can still see a historical marker by the driveway leading to former Mullenger farmstead.)

After graduating from Denison High School in 1938, seventeen-year-old Donna packed her bags and took a train to California, where she enrolled in Los Angeles City College. "She had an aunt who lived in Los Angeles," said Pat Fleshner, vice-president with the Donna Reed Foundation's board of directors. "At that time, if you were a resident of California, it didn't cost anything for tuition."

Above: Patriotism is on display along the Lincoln Highway, including this Crawford County farm near Westside. Crawford County has 915 farms, and 54 percent of the county's residents are employed in agriculture and ag-related industries, according to 2017 census data from the U.S. Department of Agriculture. *Author's collection*.

Right: Signage near this poignant monument in the Eugene Kock Memorial Park in Westside not only shares the history of the town but also salutes Westside veterans. The park was dedicated in 2018 and honors everyone from the Westside area who has served and sacrificed in the U.S. military. *Author's collection*.

Many small towns along Iowa's Lincoln Highway have a welcome sign, including Vail, "a small town with a big heart." Vail (population 532) has a number of small businesses, including the Chub Pocket, which offers specialties like Crab Rangoon pizza and serves impressive mixed drinks on Fishbowl Friday. *Author's collection.*

In her second year of college, Mullenger was voted campus queen, which led to a photo in the *Los Angeles Times*. That got her noticed and landed her a contract with MGM Studios, which changed her name to Donna Reed for her first movie, *The Get-Away*, when she was twenty.

Modern audiences often remember Reed for her role as Mary Bailey in the classic 1946 film *It's a Wonderful Life*. Reed later won an Academy Award in the 1953 movie *From Here to Eternity*. She went on to cofound her own TV production company that produced *The Donna Reed Show* on ABC television from 1958 through 1966. While Donna died of pancreatic cancer in 1986, her legacy lives on.

"Her career spanned the great American century and reflected all that was good about our country," said Reed's daughter, Mary Owen, in a tribute produced by Turner Classic Movies. "Her keen intelligence, Iowa strength, warmth and natural beauty always radiates on screen, because it was there in real life, as well."

Today, you can see a collection of photos, exhibits and more that honor this legacy at the Donna Reed Performing Arts Center and Heritage Museum in downtown Denison. Located at 1305 Broadway, this unique

Left: Movie and TV star Donna Reed (born Donna Belle Mullenger in 1921) grew up on a farm south of Denison. She played Mary Bailey in the 1946 film *It's a Wonderful Life* and later won an Academy Award in the 1953 movie *From Here to Eternity*. She also starred in *The Donna Reed Show*, on television from 1958 to 1966. *Courtesy of Donna Reed Theatre.*

Below: Photos, exhibits and other memorabilia honor Donna Reed at the Donna Reed Performing Arts Center and Heritage Museum (shown here in 2018) in downtown Denison. This unique museum (complete with a soda fountain) was originally built in 1914 as an opera house and later became a movie theater. *Author's collection.*

museum (complete with a soda fountain) was originally built in 1914 as an opera house. While the building later evolved into the Ritz movie theater, the property had fallen into disrepair by the late 1980s.

Financial donors and volunteers helped restore the distinctive building to its former glory. It's a fitting tribute to the community where a star was born. "To the Greatest Generation, Donna Reed was a sweetheart," wrote Michael Morain with the Iowa Department of Cultural Affairs. "To Baby Boomers, a mother. To many Millennials, she was a benefactor, thanks to her namesake foundation that helped launch young people's careers in the performing arts. And to Iowans, she was always one of us."

One of the places Donna would visit when she returned to her hometown was Cronk's restaurant, which had served locals and Lincoln Highway travelers since 1929. "Donna was genuine," said Eric Skoog, who owned Cronk's with his wife, Terri, for many years.

Through the years, Cronk's became a destination for not only hungry diners but also presidential hopefuls. Candidates from Joe Biden to Jesse Jackson hosted campaign events at the spacious restaurant, which included a café, lounge and a large dining room with a supper club feel. All this came to

Cronk's restaurant was an integral part of Denison from 1929 until it closed permanently in 2020. When the Lincoln Highway Association hosted its national convention in Denison in June 2017, this classic car outside of Cronk's welcomed visitors to the restaurant. *Author's collection.*

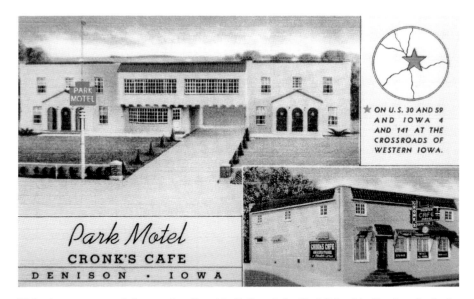

This vintage postcard shows what Cronk's Café and the Park Motel in Denison looked like back in the day. You can still check in at the Park Motel, which was built in 1940, is listed in the National Register of Historic Places and features various themed guest rooms. *Author's collection.*

The Crawford County Fair is among the best of Iowa's county fairs. Each July, local 4-H and FFA youth compete at the fairgrounds in Denison, where they showcase projects they've worked on all year, from livestock to baking, clothing and crafts. *Author's collection.*

an end, though, in 2020 during the COVID-19 pandemic, when the Skoogs decided to close the business permanently.

While you can't eat at Cronk's anymore, you can still check in across the road at the Park Motel. This Spanish Colonial Revival building built in 1940 is listed in the National Register of Historic Places. Choose from a variety of themed suites, including the Donna Reed Suite, Fisherman's Delight Room, Moose Suite, Wilderness Suite and Leopard Jacuzzi Suite.

Before you leave Denison (which also has a thriving Hispanic community and boasts a mariachi band at Denison High School), stop by the Dairy Queen just down the road from the Park Motel and order a Denison Burger (or make it a double!). I can't explain why these burgers are so good. Maybe it's the locally sourced beef. Maybe is the well-seasoned grill. Perhaps Rural Revival's website says it best: "Maybe why we really love this place is because of what the Denison Dairy Queen represents: everything we love about a small town. It's this combination of all the right things that make you walk away with a feeling that life really is good…that we really are living the American dream…that being part of a rural community really is something special. And that's exactly what keeps us coming back."

DOW HOUSE PRESERVES THE STORY OF PIONEER IOWA

As you leave Denison and head west, you'll pass the former Crawford County "poor farm," a county-run facility where people in need, primarily elderly and disabled people, were supported at public expense in years past. Just beyond the tiny town of Arion, you'll arrive in Dow City. Drive up the hill to see the beautiful Dow House, which offers a commanding view of the area.

If you let your mind wander, you can almost imagine what this property might have looked like when western Iowa was still a wild, unsettled land, just as it was when Simeon E. Dow (1821–1906) and his wife, Chloe A. Dow (1825–1906), arrived on the prairie.

A New Hampshire native, Dow had grown up in Michigan, marrying Chloe Smith in 1846 (the same year Iowa became a state). The couple moved to Iowa in 1852. By 1855, they had settled in Union Township, Crawford County, on the present site of Dow City.

Dow built a successful real estate business by purchasing land warrants from U.S. military veterans. Congress had passed a veterans benefits act in March 1855, providing land warrants to veterans of any U.S. military conflict to date. Each land warrant was redeemable in cash or in public lands. Since many eligible veterans didn't want to go west, land speculators like Dow bought up land warrants at competitive prices and exchanged them for specific tracts of land in places like western Iowa, according to "The Simeon E. Dow House—A National Historic Place," which appeared in the winter 1973 issue of the *Annals of Iowa.*

By the end of the Civil War, Dow's landholdings included 2,600 acres. While the Dow family prospered in the pioneer settlement of Dowville, Chloe was unhappy and longed to return to her friends and family back east. "Simeon told Chloe, 'If you stay, I will build you a mansion,'" said Jodi Head, office manager for Crawford County Conservation and a volunteer at the Dow House. "She agreed, and he followed through on his promise."

Dow built a two-story red brick home from 1872 to 1874 on a hill overlooking the Boyer River valley. The Dow House reportedly cost $11,000 (roughly $277,000 in 2022 dollars) at a time when most new homes in the area cost $2,000 or less.

All the bricks for the thirteen-room mansion were made on the four-acre property, which also includes a carriage house. The mansion was built to last,

When Simeon Dow and his wife, Chloe, moved in 1855 to the area that would become Dow City, western Iowa was still an unsettled land. Chloe was unhappy with pioneer life, but Simeon built her this home in 1872–74 on the south edge of town to entice her to stay, which she did. *Author's collection.*

added Head, who noted that the walls are three bricks thick, and many of the rooms have twelve-foot ceilings. It provided a comfortable home for the Dows and their three children, Chloe Alma Dow-Graves (1848–1902), Sanford Asa Dow (1856–1919) and William E. Dow (1861–1940).

For nearly thirty years, the Dow House was a focal point for much of the economic, political, social and cultural activity in the community. The first floor included a formal front parlor featuring a marble fireplace that was brought to Dow City by covered wagon, Head said. The first floor also includes a kitchen, dining room and music room, complete with a Steinway baby grand piano and massive Wurlitzer harp under the room's proscenium arch.

The library-office located just west of the elegant front doors functioned as a place to receive business callers, as a retreat for gentlemen to talk business and politics after dinner and as a private retreat for Dow, who ran the Dow & Graves store, which specialized in lumber, grain, wool, wagons and farm machinery. Dow also raised longhorn cattle, operated a cheese factory, served as the town's mayor and postmaster and helped build some of the community's first schools and churches, including the Baptist church.

There are five rooms on the second floor of the Dow House, with the large upper hall and four bedrooms, including room for the Dow family's cook and maid. After the Dow family sold the home in 1902, it passed to various owners through the years, including Head's great-grandparents Albert and Alfreda Birkhofer, who lived there in the late 1930s.

The home was later divided up into apartments and eventually fell into disrepair. By the late 1960s, the community was planning to demolish the property until local preservationists took action to save the historic home. The Crawford County Conservation Board purchased the property in 1970. With support from the Crawford County Historical Society and the Dow City community, the home was restored, added to the National Register of Historic Places in 1972 and opened to the public in 1974. "I feel so much peace here," said Head, who enjoys giving tours of the historic home.

CHEVY CREATES A ROLLING TRIBUTE TO VETERANS

When you're in the Dow City area, you might see history rolling down the road in the form of a 1955 Chevrolet Bel Air. Tom Brink of Dow City restored this car, which belonged to Private First Class Michael Heller.

Tom Brink of Dow City restored this 1955 Chevrolet Bel Air that belonged to one of his high school friends, Private First Class Michael Heller, who was killed in action in Vietnam at age nineteen in 1970. Years later, Brink found Heller's car in a junkyard, where it had been for decades. He restored the Chevy and added a mural on the trunk to pay tribute to Heller and all Vietnam veterans. *Author's collection.*

Brink attended high school with Heller, who was killed in action in Vietnam at age nineteen in 1970.

Years later, Brink found Heller's car in a junkyard, where it had been for decades. He restored the Chevy and added a mural on the trunk to pay tribute to Heller and all Vietnam veterans. The poignant message displayed on the car (with the custom license plate "FLNHERO") never fails to attract attention, whether the Chevy is displayed at a car show or rolling down the highway.

HARRISON COUNTY

While today's technology makes it easy to find your way along the Lincoln Highway, travelers who came through Harrison County in the 1800s, long before roads like the Lincoln Highway took shape, looked for landmarks like the Z.T. Dunham Pioneer Stock Farm barn.

As you approach Dunlap from the east on Highway 30, look to the south and you can spot this brick barn, which was built in 1870 by Z.T. (Zachary Taylor) Dunham to house horses. Back in Dunlap, there are some new landmarks to help you find your way, including a vibrant Lincoln Highway mural.

The story starts with Jill Schaben, thirty-seven, a Dunlap "import" and wife of Cody Schaben, whose family runs the Dunlap Livestock Auction. When Jill was visiting some of her friends in Creston, Iowa, she was inspired by some murals in the town. Schaben asked a lot of questions about those interesting murals and thought it might be fun to paint some in Dunlap. "I figured, 'How hard could it be?' Famous last words!" Schaben joked.

Schaben, who grew up on a farm near Lenox, Iowa, isn't the type to back down from a challenge. After securing some financial support from the Dunlap Community Development Corporation (DCDC), she and a small crew of local volunteers painted six murals in six months in the spring, summer and fall of 2021 in Dunlap, a town of 1,038 residents. "Ambition met funding, and Dunlap became a lot more colorful," said Schaben, a graphic designer who coordinates Dunlap's annual Art at the Park event.

Schaben started by developing ideas for potential murals. After scouting some possible locations to paint, Schaben pitched the concept to the building

As you approach Dunlap from the east on the Lincoln Highway, look to the south and you might spot the Z.T. Dunham Pioneer Stock Farm barn. Built in 1870 by Z.T. (Zachary Taylor) Dunham, the horse barn served as a landmark that guided travelers in western Iowa. *Author's collection.*

owners. Most were open to the idea. Schaben first approached Dale Smith, the owner of Smitty's Grocery at 812 Iowa Avenue. "I said I'd round up the labor and materials, and if he didn't like the mural, we'd paint it white. What do you have to lose?"

Before long, the south side of Smitty's Grocery featured a striking "sunburst" design with wide blue and white stripes, a red-and-white "Shop Local" box and a trio of colorful popsicles near the words "Dunlap, Iowa, USA." It fits the local flavor of the store, whose website reminds people that shopping at Smitty's:

- Keeps dollars in the local economy
- Creates local jobs
- Helps the environment by buying locally
- Invests in local ownership
- Utilizes the many years of Smitty's expertise in the food business

Once people saw the mural at Smitty's, others wanted one on their building, too. Greg and Monica Stinn, who own Dunlap Plumbing and

In the summer of 2021, Jill Schaben and local volunteers painted colorful murals around Dunlap, including this red, white and blue motif on a former welding shop that now features Lincoln Highway designs. *Author's collection.*

Heating, proposed a concept for a Lincoln Highway mural on their long, low-slung building (dubbed "Greg's Chevy Garage") along Highway 30. Monica drafted the idea with a pencil and paper, and Schaben digitized it for them.

The Lincoln Highway motif livens up this former welding shop, thanks to the classic red, white and blue Lincoln Highway logo, along with a handy milage report notifying motorists that it's 2,159 miles to San Francisco and 1,277 miles to New York from Dunlap.

Across from the Lincoln Highway mural, an eye-catching design adds a big pop of color to a warehouse. The "Welcome to Dunlap" greeting brings an element of fun to the back of this building used by Sullivan Supply, a livestock supply company.

During the summer of 2021, volunteers painted another mural at the community's swimming pool. Local veterans also painted a military-themed mural on the side of city hall, where the American Legion meets. Even a faded old Robin Hood Flour "ghost sign" on the side of Bonsall TV & Appliance's warehouse at the corner of Iowa Avenue and Seventh Street downtown got a new lease on life.

Two to nine volunteers usually showed up to paint the murals. "After going through the COVID-19 pandemic in 2020, we enjoyed the social aspect of bringing people together again," Schaben said. It took two to three solid days of painting to complete each mural. The volunteers used exterior latex paint purchased at Dunlap Lumber. "We wanted to buy local," Schaben said.

The materials to paint each mural cost approximately $600 to $1,000. While the DCDC helped fund the first two murals, local businesses paid for the murals that were painted on their property. "Dunlap is a great place to live, and these murals offer a fun way to beautify our town," said Schaben, who became executive director of the DCDC in March 2022.

Her contributions haven't gone unnoticed. KDSN Radio in Denison named her the Johnson Propane Citizen of the Month in January 2022. "I'm so proud of our town," she said. "There's so much going on in Dunlap, and it has so much potential. We want to ensure Dunlap is a place our kids and grandkids will want to live."

Neighbors Serving Neighbors: Dunlap Livestock Auction Thrives for Three Generations

A big part of Dunlap's economic success is connected to the local livestock auction. On sale day, the rapid-fire, rhythmic chant of the auctioneer sparks a sense of excitement and energy that's hard to replicate. The earthy smell of cattle wafts through the air as the animals file through the sale ring at the Dunlap Livestock Auction. Everyone's watching to see which cowboy hats are nodding and which buyers are flicking their index finger to bid.

Then there's the unforgettable taste of home-cooked hot-beef dinners and other comfort foods at the Bull Pen Diner on sale day. "A livestock auction is a total sensory experience, from the sights to the smells to the sounds," said Jim Schaben Jr., sixty-six, who owns the Dunlap Livestock Auction with his family.

It's an experience that has flourished weekly for decades along the Lincoln Highway/Highway 30, thanks to three generations of the Schaben family, who have owned the Dunlap Livestock Auction since 1950. "For over 70 years, this has been the place where buyers and sellers meet to participate in one of the last, true, price discovery mechanisms in the United States—the livestock auction," Schaben said. "Competitive marketing allows sellers to earn the highest possible price for their livestock in an auction setting."

When COVID-19 lockdowns prompted shutdowns of many businesses across Iowa by late March 2020, the Dunlap Livestock Auction didn't miss a

Jim Schaben Jr. owns the Dunlap Livestock Auction with his family. Since 1950, three generations of the Schaben family have owned the Dunlap Livestock Auction, which offers weekly cattle sales. *Author's collection.*

beat. "We already had a video system in place where people could view the auction from home and bid online," Schaben said.

The Dunlap Livestock Auction has long been an innovator. "We had some of the first computers and fax machines in town, back when those were new technology," Schaben said. "We've embraced change throughout our history because it allows us to do a better job for our customers."

There was a time when plenty of small towns across Iowa and beyond boasted a local livestock auction barn. That was certainly the case when Schaben's parents, Jim Sr. and Ruth, moved from Earling, Iowa, to Dunlap in 1948 to run the auction barn. "When I started in business with my parents in 1979, there were still 150 to 160 livestock sale barns across Iowa, along with the Sioux City Stockyards," Schaben said. "The 1980s Farm Crisis started a trend of livestock barns going out of business. The 1998 crash of the hog market finished it."

Today, there are fewer than forty Iowa livestock auctions, according to the Iowa Department of Agriculture and Land Stewardship. The Schaben family's commitment to the livestock auction business has helped their business grow and thrive. "I never thought about doing anything but working in the auction business," said Schaben, who majored in business at Texas State University, the alma mater of President Lyndon B. Johnson and country music superstar George Strait. "I always knew I wanted to come back home."

The Dunlap Livestock Auction has carved a niche by focusing on cattle. The regular sale day occurs every Tuesday, with the fed cattle auction starting at 9:00 a.m. More feeder cattle auctions are held on scheduled Fridays. Bred-cow cattle auctions are held on scheduled Wednesdays. "Our biggest crowds come for the bred animal sales," said Schaben, who noted the sale barn can hold 350 to 375 spectators.

The busiest sale month is January, with other active months occurring in November, December, February and March. While it's typical to sell 2,700 to 3,200 cattle per auction, this might reach 5,000 head on a busy Friday.

While the Dunlap Livestock Auction's trade territory covers an eighty-mile radius around Dunlap, the business serves customers from the Missouri border to the Minnesota border. As farms have grown larger through the years, so has the nature of cattle sales at the Dunlap Livestock Auction. "When I started in the business in 1979, a huge consigner would bring in 100 cattle, or a big buyer would purchase 100 head," Schaben said. "Now, it's not uncommon for customers to have 15,000 to 20,000 head in their feedlot, so the number of cattle we handle for buyers and sellers has grown too."

Some customers only use the auction barn once a year, while others are regulars. "When you come here every week for weeks on end, you're assigned a bid number," Schaben said. A small collection of plaques on the business office wall honors bidders whose number was retired after the customer passed away. One of the more recent ones features a photo of Ron Barnhart, who spent his life farming and working with cattle. "On April 18, 2020, the number 1100 was retired from the buyers' registration list at the Dunlap Livestock Auction," reads the plaque. "A good friend and a valued customer has been lost, but his memory will remain with us for many years to come."

This family atmosphere reflects how the Dunlap Livestock Auction is more than a critical link in the farm-to-fork connection—it's a hub of the local community. People socialize here with friends and neighbors. They gather for special events, like the World Livestock Auctioneer Championship & Auction, which the Dunlap Livestock Auction hosted on June 8, 2002. Just a year later, Jon Schaben won the 2003 World Livestock Auctioneer Championship.

While awards are great, the Schaben family is even more honored to serve generations of loyal customers. "We're proud to be a third-generation business doing business with the fourth and fifth generations of some of our customers," Schaben said. "We're also proud to work with ranches in Idaho and Oregon that my family has worked with for nearly 60 years."

Along with livestock auctions, the Schabens handle household auctions, land sales and farm sales in the area. No matter where they go, they aren't afraid to promote their hometown of Dunlap, from its nine-hole golf course to its new housing subdivision to classic restaurants like the Gold Slipper, where customers often head after a successful day at the sale barn. "Dunlap has just over 1,000 residents, but we're progressive for a little town," Schaben said.

While Schaben is at the age when many people retire, that doesn't interest him. "I still enjoy the auction business and plan to keep going."

Welcome to Woodbine, Home of the Famous Brick Streets

When you head west from Dunlap and arrive in Woodbine, be sure to turn onto Lincolnway, so you can drive on a piece of American history. While the street was originally named Vail Street, the city changed the name to Lincolnway as the Lincoln Highway became more popular.

In 1921, the town transformed the hard, packed-dirt street into a bricked street. In fact, Woodbine laid bricks along Lincolnway and throughout the commercial district—thirty-five blocks in all. Time has shown that brick streets last decades longer than concrete streets. Local residents have supported preservation efforts through the years to save the iconic pavers, including two major rehabilitation projects in 2003 and 2019. "A few grumps complain the streets are noisy or not as smooth for drivers, but many residents view them as a beautiful, cultural asset and a nice way to slow down traffic," according to new Lincoln Highway signage.

In 2011, the Woodbine Lincoln Highway and Brick Street Historic District were added to the National Register of Historic Places, thanks to the downtown's iconic Iowa commercial architecture and the longest original bricked section of the Lincoln Highway in Iowa.

This milestone built on the momentum that had started in 2008, when Woodbine was designated a Main Street Iowa community. This state program works with a select group of communities that successfully complete a competitive application process and commit to exceptionally high standards for downtown economic development. A collective push in 2008 helped Woodbine assemble a team of community leaders, including small-business owners, bankers, real estate and development professionals, local government officials, educators, farmers, retirees and hometown volunteers. "Ten business vacancies and the threat of two historic buildings falling in the street in a heap motivated the team," said Deb Sprecker, executive director of Woodbine Main Street. "This led to some pretty amazing results."

Volunteers went to work restoring the community's historic downtown. Sometimes that meant replacing old windows with energy-efficient ones. In other cases, it meant installing geothermal heating and cooling systems. For other properties, it involved a complete renovation. "Rural revitalization is a team sport," Sprecker said. "It takes a willingness to embrace big ideas, and it requires a lot of cooperation and trust."

In 2014, Woodbine received a National Great American Main Street Award for "generating economic vitality, fostering a unique sense of place, and planning the community's future," according to the National Trust for Historic Preservation.

By 2020, a snapshot of Woodbine's before-and-after story included more than $10 million invested downtown through private and public funding sources, more than twenty-eight buildings rehabbed (either with total restorations or exterior façades), thirty-six upper-story units added to the district and an increase in total assessed property values in Main Street's three-block footprint up $2.5 million.

In 2022, Woodbine also made headlines for bringing 150 new homes to town. The neighborhood, Harvest Hills at Woodbine, will be connected to the rest of the town by the new Community, Recreation, Education, Wellness (CREW) Center, which includes a gymnasium, fitness facility and track, aquatics facility, classrooms and community meeting space.

GRAIN ELEVATOR SHOWCASES SPECTACULAR PUBLIC ART

With all this recent progress, it's easy to forget that Woodbine's ability to redefine what's possible for small-town Iowa began to take root in an unlikely place—an old grain elevator by the railroad tracks on the edge of town. While most people saw a decrepit building that should be torn down, Sprecker saw potential. "Right after we moved to town in 2005, Woodbine's city council approached my husband, Trent, about cleaning up that site," she said.

Trent was the new general manager of United Western, a farmer-owned cooperative (now part of Heartland Cooperative) that owned the site. He understood the city council's request, as he also likes neat, tidy facilities. It wouldn't be too hard to get rid of some old grain bins and sheds around there, but the seventy-two-foot-tall elevator was another issue.

The wooden, "milk carton"–style elevator had been built in 1948, with hundreds of two-by-six-inch boards nailed together. "It contained nine vertical bins and was built to last," said Gaylin Swift, seventy-two, who worked for the local co-op for thirty-three years before retiring in 2016.

This wooden "milk carton"–style elevator built in 1948 in Woodbine is now a piece of art, complete with a forty-five-foot-tall metal corn stalk. This larger-than-life sculpture was installed in 2011, along with vibrant LED lights that illuminate the elevator each night. *Author's collection.*

The elevator hadn't been used since the 1980s or early 1990s, though, and was steadily deteriorating. Still, it was a landmark in the community. One day, when the Spreckers were driving home from church, Deb looked again at the time-worn structure and turned to Trent. "Honey, you can't tear torn that old elevator," she said. "There's too much potential there."

While the co-op's farmer-led board of directors were skeptical, they agreed to sell the elevator to the city for one dollar. By then, Sprecker had been floating an idea—"Hey, anyone want to save that grain elevator?"—at a local meeting or two. "People didn't know yet about my crazy ideas, and a number of them said, 'Sure, why not?'" she joked.

The idea brought back happy memories for some local residents, she added. "I'll never forget one lady's story of how much she loved riding along with her grandpa in his truck when he'd go to the co-op because he bought her a grape pop."

Other residents had grown their careers there. "I spent hours working in that elevator," recalled Swift, a Woodbine-area native who bagged feed for area livestock farmers.

Other community members were historic preservationists who didn't want to lose a distinctive part of Woodbine's heritage. "The community wanted to save the elevator because so many other wooden elevators in the Midwest have been torn down and lost forever," Sprecker said. "Woodbine rallied around this project."

Community members started putting ideas on paper when they participated in Iowa's Living Roadways Community Visioning Program. Sponsored by the Iowa Department of Transportation, this program provides small Iowa communities with the planning and design resources needed to make meaningful transportation improvements to the local landscape. Students from Iowa State University's (ISU) Department of Landscape Architecture work with program participants to create transportation enhancement plans reflecting the values and identity of the community.

"By 2008/2009, if you had a shovel-ready project, which we did by then, funding sources and grants were available to help make your plans a reality," Sprecker noted.

These partnerships and financial resources helped support a cleanup of the area, remodeling on the elevator façade and a community-guided design process to determine what art to include on the structure. "We only had 90 days to come up with a design," Sprecker said. "People suggested putting a cuckoo clock on the elevator, turning it into a climbing wall or making it look like a rocket ship." The community finally agreed on a field with contour farming strips, a conservation practice that protects soil and water quality. The design also honors the unique formation of wind-deposited soil in the nearby Loess (pronounced "luss") Hills, located in parts of western Iowa near the Missouri River.

The next challenge involved finding a company that could handle such a large-scale art installation. While Sprecker called some local metal shops, no one wanted to tackle a project of this size. "I was getting a little panicky," she admitted. Then she connected with TMCO, a manufacturing company in Lincoln, Nebraska, that was expanding. When Sprecker showed them pictures of the Woodbine elevator and explained the project, they agreed to sign on.

It helped that a recent TMCO hire, Emily Broderson, was already familiar with the elevator. She had been part of the Living Roadways Community Visioning Program for Woodbine when she was an ISU student. She designed the grain elevator artwork, which includes a forty-five-foot-tall, rust-colored, metal corn stalk ("a lovely, lyrical design of a cornstalk," as Sprecker noted), set inside a rectangular metal frame with a colorful green- and white-striped field in the background.

This larger-than-life "sculpture," which was installed in 2011, proves that art has the power to transform, inspire and illuminate. Vibrant LED lights on the elevator have added a sense of drama each night since Woodbine hosted a grand lighting ceremony in 2011.

For the ceremony, local elementary school children made their own ears of corn out of clear plastic pop bottles that were covered in yellow tissue paper and lit from inside with a glow stick. After gathering at the Woodbine Main Street office, which is housed in former gas station built in 1928, a few hundred kids and adults marched up the street to the grain elevator and sang an Iowa song as part of the ceremony. "The grain elevator has become a real point of pride for the community," said Sprecker, who noted that photos of the distinctive structure often appear on promotional materials not only for Woodbine but also for Iowa as a whole.

Like the elevator itself, the artwork and lighting are meant to endure. "We wanted the artwork to be as sustainable as possible, so it's designed to last at least 20 years without requiring any maintenance," Sprecker said. "The energy-efficient LED lights mean we won't have to change the light bulbs for a long time either."

In the summer, wildflowers blooming in the foreground add little pops of color to this striking landmark. For Swift, who has seen the elevator transform from a dusty workplace to a blight on the skyline to elegant artwork, the project symbolizes the spirit of Woodbine itself. "As a community, we've been fortunate. The town, like this old elevator, has evolved."

STAY GROUNDED: BUILDING GROUNDS, HEAVY METAL RENAISSANCE REVITALIZE WOODBINE

Some say that good ideas start with brainstorming. Others know that great ideas start with coffee. That's true at the Building Grounds coffee shop in downtown Woodbine, where coffee, art, creativity and conversation are always brewing. "I love how coffee brings people together," said Nikki Davis, who co-owns and manages Building Grounds in the front of the shop at 415 Walker Street, while her husband, Jefferson ("Jeff"), runs the Heavy Metal Renaissance welding shop in the back.

Each weekday morning from 6:30 a.m. to 11:00 a.m., a unique mix of customers stops by Building Grounds. Some are teachers heading to work at the local school. Others are Woodbine Community School students. Some customers work at Woodbine Manufacturing Company, a local factory that makes Tommy Gate hydraulic liftgates for trucks and vans.

In the warmer months, Building Grounds attracts people from the nearby Willow Lake Recreation Area, a popular fishing, camping and kayaking destination. Some of the most reliable patrons year round are the retirees (including ninety-eight-year-old "Mama Lou") who gather every morning to catch up on the latest news.

Then there's Mike Jensen, Woodbine's chief of police, who is also a farrier (a specialist who trims and shoes horses' hooves). "He used to say, 'Men don't drink coffee through a straw!' and was strictly a traditional coffee guy," Nikki said. "Now he enjoys an occasional 'foo foo' coffee."

Among the top-selling "foo foo" coffees at Building Grounds are Caramelvicious (with two types of caramel, two types of chocolate and a hit of vanilla, available as a latte, frappe, steamer, smoothie or over ice), Cherry Bomb (like a chocolate-covered cherry in a cup, with or without caffeine), Ballroom Blitz (a great option if you want caffeine but don't like the flavor of espresso) and Peanut Butter Twix (dark chocolate, caramel and real peanut butter blended into a filling drink with a kick). "I have a syrup addiction," Nikki confessed. "I went from just four flavors to not having enough counter space for all the flavors."

Coffee, art and conversation are always brewing at Building Grounds coffee shop in downtown Woodbine. On a February morning in 2022 (*left to right*), Donna Pape, Building Grounds owner Nikki Davis, Louretta "Mama Lou" Waite and Sharron Kindred gathered to catch up on the news of the day. *Author's collection.*

Nikki never imagined that she and her husband would become business owners in Woodbine. She was a city girl from Omaha who thought it might be interesting to live in a small town someday. Jeff grew up in the small town of Crescent, Iowa, along the Lincoln Highway.

After the couple married, they settled in Modale, Iowa, a small town in western Harrison County. Jeff worked as a union welder with the Local 3 in Omaha, where he specialized in commercial metal fabrication. Life changed quickly, however, when the Missouri River flooded areas near Modale in the late spring of 2011. "The flooding was so bad that the U.S. Army Corps of Engineers told us to get out," Nikki said. "We were flood evacuees at a rock-bottom point in our lives."

The Davis family moved to a rental house on the other side of Harrison County in Woodbine. The longer they stayed, the more they liked the town. "There's at least one of everything here, including a dentist, doctor's office, grocery store, restaurant, school, pharmacy and more," said Nikki, who was working at the *Woodbine Twiner* newspaper office. "You've got all the basics you need, with small-town vibes."

Some of those basics suffered, though, when a fire swept through downtown Woodbine in late September 2013, just a few days before the town's annual Applefest celebration, which generally brings about 10,000 people to the town of 1,500. A strong southwest wind spread the blaze, which consumed two storefronts and caused severe smoke damage to nearby businesses. Many residents were concerned that this major setback might be more than the town could handle.

Undeterred, local economic development leaders applied for grants to save the historic façades damaged in the fire and construct new buildings behind them. "Woodbine people work miracles, and they always rally for each other," Nikki said.

Civic leaders put out a request for proposals for what those "now-new" buildings could become. People submitted applications, including Nikki, who proposed an art gallery and a coffee shop. "I gave myself a headache trying to write my first-ever business proposal and figure out the financials," said Nikki, who received an Open for Business grant through Main Street Iowa and worked with a local lender to obtain a loan.

Nikki became Woodbine's local barista when Building Grounds debuted in 2016. Her shop opened a colorful new chapter in the story of this historic property, which was built around 1884 to house one of the town's first pharmacies.

Jeff also took a leap of faith around this time. He was shocked by the tragic death of Kerrie Orozco, twenty-nine, an Omaha police officer. This mother of two, with her newborn still in the neonatal intensive care unit, was shot and killed as she helped serve a felony arrest warrant on a known gang member. Jeff felt compelled to do something—anything. He lived on Monster energy drinks and stayed up for three days to build a tribute to Orozco—a giant replica of an Omaha Police Department badge that barely fit into his family's tiny garage.

As news of the remarkable badge spread, the Davis family saw how the tribute impacted others, especially Orozco's fellow police officers. "We realized that art is able to say so much without saying a word," Nikki said.

As Jeff continued to create more beautiful things from his makeshift workshop in the garage, he knew that he needed more space. Ultimately, he decided to leave his union job of twenty years to open Heavy Metal Renaissance Art Gallery in Woodbine, serving as the gallery's resident artist. "It's a terrifying leap to become self-employed, but it has been good," Jeff said.

Today, he creates a wide array of commissioned projects, from larger-than-life metal fish to an oversized, sparkling purple guitar inspired by the music of Prince. Some of these creations have become public art displays in Woodbine—as well as in Mankato, Minnesota; Sioux Falls, South Dakota; and Lincoln, Nebraska—while others are displayed at Building Grounds. "We planned the gallery as part of the shop from the beginning," said Jeff, who was inspired by the Artists' Cooperative Gallery, a space located in Omaha's historic Old Market that showcases various artists' work.

The gallery at Building Grounds displays local artists' creations, from postcards and woodworking to metal sculptures made from recycled items, including a 1941 Cadillac fender skirt. A huge Pottawattamie County sheriff badge that Jeff built as a tribute for fallen officer Mark Burbridge stands tall near the couches where the morning coffee crowd gathers. "We back the blue," said Nikki, a self-taught AutoCAD drafter who helps out at Heavy Metal Renaissance, where Jeff is teaching her how to weld.

"We Want to Do as Much Good as Possible"

Other members of the Davis family also contribute to the business. The couple's young daughter, Eva, has been selling her own artistic creations at Building Grounds since she was in grade school.

Step into the welding shop and you might see Bon Bon Sewer Cat, a sleek brown tabby who likes to sleep under a bench when she's not roaming over to the Casey's convenience store or the Dairy Sweet for a treat. (During her adventures, Bon Bon tries to avoid Frank, an equally friendly gray and white cat that is also a fixture in downtown Woodbine.)

Whether it's the cats, the metal art or the coffee, there's always something to talk about at Building Grounds. Nikki looks for novel ways to market the businesses, including popular "Tattoos and Tarot" events, complete with food, coffee, wine, wine slushies, music, tattoos and tarot card readings. She also creates promotions connected to events like Read Across America in early March around Dr. Seuss's birthday. For 2022, she served up "Moose Moss," a white chocolate and coconut latte that was tinted green and named for Thidwick the Big-Hearted Moose, from the classic Dr. Seuss children's book.

"We're a small, family-owned business giving everything we've got to serve others," Nikki said. "We want to do as much good as possible along the way."

BE THE GOOD: WOODBINE'S GOOD FELLOWS SERVES FINE FOOD AND FELLOWSHIP

Chance favors the bold, especially when you run a small business. Just ask Todd Waite, co-owner of Good Fellows in Woodbine. "We've made it our goal to be the best restaurant between Omaha and Des Moines."

It's definitely a bold goal for a restaurateur in a farming community of 1,500 people. Yet the Good Fellows team dreams no little dreams. I could sense this as soon as I stepped inside the door, where a chalkboard lists daily specials for Wok'N Wednesday, Pasta & Wine on Thursday, a Sunday buffet and more.

While Good Fellows has become known for exceptional food, there are signs—literally—of something more profound going on here. Head down the hallway to the Lodge Room (a popular place for parties and other gatherings), and one sign reads, "A horse after the race is won, a dog when the hunt is over, a bee with its honey stored, and a human being after helping others. Be the good."

Head back to the bar, and there's another large black sign over the kitchen doorway. "To the Good Fellows, the group of anonymous, silent partners and volunteers who made this restaurant possible. Good Fellows believe that if more of us valued food and cheer and song over hoarded gold, the world would be a happier place. This club is dedicated to them and all those who share this belief."

It all makes sense when you know that Good Fellows is a story of second chances and the powerful ways food can connect a community. "I like us identifying as the underdog," said Waite, thirty-seven, a Woodbine native. "We've got something to prove."

In many ways, Good Fellows mirrors the mission of the Independent Order of Odd Fellows (IOOF), whose local Odd Fellows Lodge 405 met in the building for years until the group disbanded sometime in the 1980s (as best as anyone can remember). The IOOF, an international fraternal order, gets right to the point on its website:

Do you want to help make your community a better place and help those in need?

Have you been searching for a way to help others and be a part of something bigger than yourself?

If you answered yes, you don't just fit the IOOF—you fit at Good Fellows, which opened after an earlier restaurant closed in 2017 following a two-year stint. "A restaurant isn't a hierarchy, it's a collaboration," said Waite, a 2003 Woodbine High School graduate. "The way you treat people matters."

As Waite and the restaurant's supporters regrouped, they followed the Odd Fellows' philosophy of working together to help others and become a part of something bigger than themselves. "We literally called people and asked them to donate to help support the new restaurant—and they did," said Waite, as he visited with me in the dining room one February afternoon in 2022 after the noon rush was over.

When Good Fellows opened in 2018, it ushered in a whole new mindset. "The closure of the other restaurant was such a dramatic thing that it allowed us to make some big changes," Waite said. "We treat everyone here like Good Fellows."

The momentum for change didn't start only with Good Fellows. It began taking root around 2008, when the community started working together to revitalize downtown Woodbine. An extensive remodeling project from 2008 to 2011 helped transform the future Good Fellows building at 501 Walker Street from a tired, timeworn place into an inviting space.

Through the years, this distinctive building had housed a bank, Sieble's Department Store, the Nicely Shoe Store, Hyde Furniture Store, Moore

Housed in a former downtown building where the local Lodge 405 of the Independent Order of Odd Fellows (IOOF) met for decades, Good Fellows is redefining what's possible with a small-town restaurant. Among the crew (shown here in March 2022, *left to right*) are Jack Cue, Sara Marsh, Todd Waite, Rene Hiller, Juan Rosa, Skylyr Wohlers, Kevin Risdal, Judd Kirk and Mike Ackerson. *Author's collection.*

Bros. Super Market and Bob's Café. Large windows that had been covered up during the 1970s energy crisis were restored to offer panoramic views of downtown Woodbine. "We have this amazing building and wanted to make the most of it," Waite said.

Whether you enter through the corner entrance or the side door on Fifth Street, Good Fellows feels like you're stepping back in time to a place that's steeped in history, yet also on the cutting edge. Countless details remind you that this building, constructed in 1878, was once an Odd Fellows lodge. (This explains the "Odd Fellows" sign on the men's restroom door and the "Rebekahs" sign on the women's restroom, since the Rebekahs were the ladies' branch of the IOOF.)

The dining room showcases vintage photos of Woodbine, along with dramatic wainscoting made of large, metal sheets with abstract, cutout shapes. (Those cool designs are remnants from Woodbine Manufacturing Company, a local factory that makes the Tommy Gate brand of hydraulic liftgates for trucks and vans). Some of the wooden benches in the main dining room were salvaged from the local Presbyterian church before it was torn down.

This spirit of innovation and transformation at Good Fellows is evident throughout Woodbine, from a new, multimillion-dollar wellness center to IGNITE Pathways, a career and technical education center designed to create hands-on learning experiences for students while they prepare for careers in health sciences; business; agriculture; food and natural resources; arts and information solutions; human services; and technology, engineering and manufacturing.

"We decided as a community that either we'll be proactive, or we'll be passive and suffer the fate that has befallen many other small, rural towns, where school enrollment is dropping, downtown buildings are empty and people are moving away," Waite said.

Taste the "World's Best Bread Pudding" and More

Waite was one of those people who left rural Iowa but chose to return. "Growing up here, I liked the opportunity to participate in lots of things. You can try sports, band, vocal music, theater and more. This helps you become a well-rounded person."

It's sometimes hard to recognize the value of these small-town advantages, though, when you're young and want to explore the world. After high school, Waite studied philosophy and English literature at the University of Northern Iowa (UNI). He didn't have a clear career path. Then the Iraq War started. "I wanted to serve and saw there were other options than the military," he said.

Waite joined the Peace Corps and spent two years in Mongolia teaching English. "There's no education like travel," he said.

It was a frustrating experience at first. The students didn't seem motivated to learn. Unable to break through to them, Waite reached out to one of his UNI professors for advice. "Todd, your students sound a lot like mine," he said. The professor urged Waite to not just focus on classroom lessons but to get to know the students. "That meant learning their names and finding out what interested them about learning English," said Waite, who started an English club. "I wanted them to know I cared."

After that, things started changing for the better. It's a lesson Waite didn't forget after he returned to Woodbine and decided to work in the restaurant business. "I kept thinking, 'What's your life for?' I wanted to do more than just make money to pay the bills."

He started to find the answers at Good Fellows. Moving far beyond a flat top and a fryer, the restaurant's skilled team has mastered the art of preparing midwestern comfort food with a twist. "It's fun to be creative, and there are endless possibilities with food," Waite said.

The team includes co-owner Mike Ackerson, who prepares one of Good Fellows' signature desserts, dubbed "the world's best bread pudding" with praline sauce. Then there's Kevin Risdal, who has served as Good Fellows' pastry chef since 2017. He loves how baking is an art and a science. "Breads are my favorite," said Risdal, a graduate of the Escoffier Culinary School. "I also like making cakes and ice cream."

Risdal, who lived in Colorado and San Diego, California, before moving back to his home state of Iowa, also takes inspiration from his kitchen colleagues, like Chef Juan Rosa. "If Juan is making something Mediterranean, I'll play off of that," said Risdal, who began his twenty-plus-year restaurant career as a dish washer and worked his way up. "That's what is fun about Good Fellows. It's something out of the ordinary."

Many of the Good Fellows' employees have stories that are out of the ordinary. Consider Chef Rosa, twenty-one. When he began working part time in the restaurant business at age fifteen, he started as a dish washer and advanced to fry cook within a week. "Right then I knew I liked cooking," said Rosa, who grew up in Woodbine.

When he landed a job at the famed Twisted Tail Steakhouse & Saloon in nearby Beebeetown, Iowa, the fast pace didn't deter him. "It only fueled my addiction for this business. I thrive under pressure and love the rush."

Waite urged Rosa, who wasn't a big fan of traditional education options, to consider culinary school. Rosa enrolled in Metropolitan Community College's Institute for the Culinary Arts in Omaha, which has been rated one of the best culinary programs in America. "I was the first person in my family to go to college," said Rosa, who continued to work at Good Fellows, where he could try out the culinary techniques he was learning in school.

While Rosa originally thought he'd like to switch to an urban, high-volume restaurant setting, he saw more opportunities close to home at Good Fellows. He enjoys coordinating five-course, prix fixe menus, along with wine pairings. "I have so much creative freedom here," said Rosa, who graduated from culinary school in November 2021. "I love what I do and want to see how much I can help elevate the small-town restaurant."

This big-picture thinking drives the team at Good Fellows, which is known for:

- DELIVERY SERVICES. Since 2018, Good Fellows has offered home delivery, something that's rare in rural towns the size of Woodbine. People around the area also look forward to Good Fellows' food truck and appreciate Good Fellows' at-home meal kits.
- HOME-GROWN BUTCHER SHOP. Good Fellows started its own butcher shop in the summer of 2021. "The COVID-19 pandemic showed everyone the importance of having a safe, reliable, local food supply," Waite said. Good Fellows contracts with local farmers who raise beef and pork. When the Good Fellows crew needs beef for hamburgers or other dishes, for example, they grind the meat in-house. Customers can also buy ground chuck from Good Fellows. "We call it 'Butcher at the Bar,'" Waite said. This reflects Good Fellows' willingness to pivot during times of change to remain competitive. "If someone has a decent idea, let's try it," Waite said.
- PUTTING PEOPLE FIRST. High turnover is common in the restaurant business, and this only accelerated during the COVID-19 pandemic in 2020–21. By February 2021, the Iowa Restaurant Association was projecting a 15 to 20 percent permanent closure rate for Iowa restaurants due to the pandemic. "Everyone instantly felt this vulnerability," Waite said. Good Fellows has managed to retain 80 percent of its staff, however, since the restaurant opened in 2018. "During the pandemic, we pooled the tip jar and shared the money with our employees who couldn't be here during the COVID-19 pandemic," said Waite, who noted that Good Fellows has four full-time and two dozen part-time employees. "We stuck together."

Customers are also sticking with Good Fellows, Waite added. "People see that good things are happening here. Woodbine proves there's still opportunity in a small town."

If you've been inspired by your visit to Woodbine, there are more great stories ahead on the Lincoln Highway. In Logan, the county seat of Harrison County, history abounds downtown. In Logan's town park near the basketball courts, wording on the eye-catching band shell built in 1947 notes that the structure is "dedicated to the men and women who served in the armed forces in World War 2."

Above: Located in Logan's town park near the basketball courts, this historic band shell was built in 1947 for $2,300 (nearly $30,000 in 2022 dollars). The Logan Chamber of Commerce and other local residents helped pay for the ball shell (shown here in March 2022), which is dedicated to the men and women who served in the armed forces in World War II. *Author's collection.*

Left: On September 1, 1928, thousands of Boy Scouts fanned out along the Lincoln Highway from coast to coast in towns like Logan and installed these small concrete markers with a small bust of Abraham Lincoln. Other traces of Lincoln Highway history abound in Logan, including a Lincoln Highway control station sign about a block from the marker. *Author's collection.*

One of the fun parts of any road trip is to look for the quirky local landmarks and attractions along the route, including this goofy guy promoting the Ultra No-Touch Car Wash in downtown Logan. *Author's collection.*

The Harrison County Historical Village and Welcome Center east of Missouri Valley is filled with interactive Lincoln Highway history. It also includes the Harrison County Freedom Rock, historic buildings, a gift shop and more. *Author's collection.*

At an intersection near the park, you can still see a 1928 Lincoln Highway marker. On September 1, 1928, thousands of Boy Scouts fanned out along the Lincoln Highway from coast to coast in towns like Logan and installed these small concrete markers featuring a small bust of Abraham Lincoln.

Other traces of Lincoln Highway history are evident in downtown Logan, including a Lincoln Highway control station sign on a brick building about a block from the marker. Control station signs were once commonplace on the Lincoln Highway, plus they were useful in an era when maps were rare and GPS was unknown. The concept of control stations was introduced in the 1918 *Complete Official Road Guide of the Lincoln Highway,* according to the Indiana Lincoln Highway Association. Control stations at various points along the highway helped motorists keep an accurate check on their mileage, allowing them to measure their exact distance from their destination (or the next community on the Lincoln Highway).

From Logan, it's only about five miles to the Harrison County Historical Village and Welcome Center, just east of Missouri Valley. This is a treasure-trove of interactive Lincoln Highway history. Take selfies by the fun exhibits, check out the gift stop, see the Harrison County Freedom Rock and more.

JC's Dairy Den Offers a Classic Taste of Iowa

Hungry yet? Cruise over to JC's Dairy Den in Missouri Valley. From its red, white and blue exterior to its time-honored menu items like fried pork tenderloins, you can truly enjoy a taste of Iowa here. "We get quite a few people stopping by in the summer who are traveling the Lincoln Highway," said Susan Cates of Magnolia, Iowa, who has owned JC's Dairy Den with her husband, James, since 2016.

Just don't expect to sit down inside at a booth or table. You can go through the drive-thru or walk up to the window to order. You can take your food to go or sit on a picnic bench nearby. "While this is how our business has always run, it saved us when the COVID-19 pandemic lockdowns stopped dine-in eating at restaurants in 2020," Cates said.

You can even ride a horse through the drive-thru, like local 4-H and FFA livestock exhibitors do around the third week in July when the Harrison County Fair gets underway. "I like fair week," said Cates, noting that the fairgrounds are practically right across the road from JC's Dairy Den.

Just like the county fair, JC's Dairy Den is one of those summertime classics that's been part of the culture here for decades. The business dates

JC's Dairy Den has been a beloved part of Missouri Valley since the 1950s. Among its signature items are Twin Bing Tornadoes, where crushed Twin Bing candies (made by the Palmer Candy Company in Sioux City, Iowa) are blended into swirls of soft-serve ice cream, along with a shot of black cherry flavoring. *Author's collection.*

back to 1954, when a local entrepreneur named Jennie Hiller started the Dairy Den. When she tried to hire a local contractor to build her new shop, he wasn't interested. "He told her she'd just be wasting her money, because a business like that would never work," Cates said.

Undeterred, Hiller asked a relative to build her little restaurant. The new business thrived, and Hiller ran it until 1965. In its sixty-eight-year history, JC's Dairy Den has had relatively few owners. Bob and Ann Huebner ran it from 1965 to 1983, followed by Ernie Weide from 1983 to 1985. Then James Cates's cousin Darrel Cates and his wife owned it from 1985 to 2016 before selling it to James and Susan Cates.

Like many successful, independently owned eateries, JC's Dairy Den is a family affair. James makes the giant, breaded, fried pork tenderloin sandwiches, along with the barbecued pork sandwiches. The Cateses also make a loose-meat sandwich that has satisfied generations of locals. "As far as I know, we're still serving the shop's original recipe," said Cates, who grew up near Crescent, just down the road on the Lincoln Highway.

While JC's Dairy Den also sells a lot of pizza burgers, they don't have a grill, so they don't serve hamburgers. They do have a fryer, though, so if you like corn dogs and other fried treats, you're in luck.

Speaking of treats, don't forget the ice cream. Along with basics like cones, shakes and malts, JC's Dairy Den is the place to go if you want a little something extra. Take the Twin Bing Tornadoes, for example. Like any good ice cream shop, JC's Dairy Den can mix crushed candies into swirls of soft-serve ice cream (hence the name "Tornado"). The Twin Bing Tornado is special, though, since it features the Twin Bing Bar, along with a shot of black cherry flavoring in the ice cream.

The roots of the Twin Bing date back nearly a century. Created in 1923, this midwestern favorite comes from the Palmer Candy Company in Sioux City, Iowa, where these candies are produced by hand. The chewy, cherry-flavored nougat candies coated with a mixture of chopped peanuts and chocolate made the top ten list of "Candy Bars Worth Crossing State Lines For," which appeared on the site Chowhound.com in 2007.

If you're lactose intolerant, fear not. JC's Dairy Den also serves DOLE Whips®. These classic dairy-free desserts are available in a variety of tempting flavors, from raspberry to orange (or twists, if you like).

If you're parched and want a pop (Iowans don't call it "soda") with a little soda fountain flair, just ask for a Cherry Pepsi. JC's Dairy Den won't fill your glass with some premade formula. You'll appreciate the bold, satisfying flavor that comes from the homemade mix of cola and cherry syrup.

Want to make your own concoction, whether it's a beverage or ice cream treat? "If you can tell us what's in it and we have the ingredients on hand, we can make it," Cates said.

These kinds of things keep people coming back for more, whether they are locals or they make the drive from Council Bluffs or Omaha. For graduates of Missouri Valley High School who have moved to other communities and states through the years, the all-school reunion weekend in the summer isn't complete without a stop at JC's Dairy Den.

After all, many of these folks landed their first part-time jobs at JC's Dairy Den, which continues to hire local students. While JC's Dairy Den shuts down in the heart of winter, it opens in mid-February or early March and stays open until the Sunday before Halloween. Sometimes the Cateses choose to shut down temporarily in the early or latter parts of the season, depending on the weather. "If the school closes due to bad weather, then we close, since most of our employees are high school kids," Susan said.

Otherwise, JC's Dairy Den is open seven days a week, starting at 11:00 a.m. Monday through Saturday and noon on Sunday. Closing time varies by the season. In the colder months, JC's Dairy Den stays open until 7:00 p.m. In the summer, it's open until 10:00 p.m.

For one couple, JC's Dairy Den became more than a place to eat—it became their wedding venue. "They went on dates here and decided to get married here several years ago, which was fun," Cates said. "We're proud to be a landmark in Missouri Valley. We love meeting people and hearing stories about their memories of the Dairy Den."

DIY Fruit Whip

Try this dairy-free dessert anytime you feel like adding a little sweetness to your day. This DIY Fruit Whip is reminiscent of the version at JC's Dairy Den.

1 cup ripe pineapple, chopped and frozen
1 ripe banana, peeled and frozen
2½ teaspoons powdered sugar
½ cup unsweetened coconut milk (or substitute vanilla ice cream, if you like)
1 teaspoon lemon or lime juice

Combine all ingredients in a blender or food processor. Cover; blend until smooth, about 2–3 minutes. Garnish with fresh pineapple. Serve immediately.

RECIPE TIPS: Use a powerful blender for best results, since frozen pineapple and banana can be hard to pulse. If you have a regular blender, let the fruit thaw slightly before blending. To get that famous swirl on your whip, freeze the mixture for about 30 to 40 minutes and then transfer the mixture to a piping bag with a 1M open star piping tip. Not a pineapple lover? You can make this whip with any frozen fruit, including strawberry, lemon, orange, raspberry and mango. Want to convert your whip into a float? Simply fill a glass halfway with fruit juice, add your fruit whip and top it all off with a maraschino cherry.

POTTAWATTAMIE COUNTY

By the time you cross into Pottawattamie County, you are entering an area that's been well traveled even before Iowa became a state in 1846. The Mormon Pioneer National Historic Trail, which runs through Pottawattamie County, traces the route that Brigham Young and his followers took when relocating the headquarters for the Church of Jesus Christ of Latter-day Saints.

On June 14, 1846, thousands of these pioneers reached Council Bluffs, then known as Kanesville. Here they created the Grand Encampment, which included more than ninety cluster settlements within a forty-mile radius of Council Bluffs. They stayed in the area for a time before continuing their journey west, according to the Council Bluffs Convention and Visitors Bureau.

When you're in this part of Pottawattamie County, there's no doubt you're in the Loess Hills, especially as the Lincoln Highway gently twists and turns along the bluffs. The Loess Hills are a rare natural wonder formed eons ago by wind-blown soil. Shaanxi, China, is the only other location where loess layers are this deep and extensive, according to the U.S. Geological Survey.

As you come around a bend on the Lincoln Highway, you'll see the Aeroplane Inn, a classic roadhouse. While it seems like it's in the middle of nowhere, it's in Honey Creek, an unincorporated community in Pottawattamie County.

"The Old Lincoln Highway is a scenic byway second to none, and our region is blessed with some of the most beautiful stretches winding through

Above: Years ago, some of the most challenging parts of the Lincoln Highway to drive in Iowa were in Pottawattamie County, near the Loess Hills. The part of the highway shown here (the "Honey Creek hill cut") could be especially difficult during inclement weather, when dirt roads turned to mud. *Courtesy of University of Michigan Library.*

Opposite: The Aeroplane Inn (shown here in March 2022) has been a classic roadhouse along the Lincoln Highway for decades. While it seems like it's in the middle of nowhere, it's technically in Honey Creek, an unincorporated community in Pottawattamie County. *Author's collection.*

the Loess Hills and along the Missouri River floodplain," noted Greg Jerrett, who has written a number of Nightlife Review articles for the *Omaha World Herald*. "Posited here between aesthetically pleasing and functional is a classic roadhouse, the Aeroplane Inn. Thus named for its former resemblance to an airplane, generations of Roadites would drive a country mile or 50 to tear it up in the pub then jump and jive in the hangar-sized dance hall to everything from Hank Williams to T-Bone Walker."

While the Aeroplane Inn's dance hall burned down years ago, the roadhouse remains, offering hospitality, beverages and comfort food to locals, tourists, bikers, cyclists, campers and others. Some are attracted by the sign outside promising the "coldest beer in town." Others come in for the appetizers (ranging from breaded mushrooms to tater tots), pizza, chicken wings, burgers and Taco Thursday. Sports fans stop by to watch big games like Iowa/Nebraska football. Still others just want to take their order outside the Aeroplane Inn and enjoy the view, especially when the weather is inviting. "Outside is a covered beer garden," Jerrett wrote in his 2018 article "Aeroplane Inn Offers a Trip Back in Time." "There's nothing nicer

than sitting outside looking out over the floodplain as the sun sets and the lightning bugs come out."

Just down the road, another destination worth visiting is the Hitchcock Nature Center, which offers recreational opportunities that foster greater appreciation and understanding of the Loess Hills. The Hitchcock Nature Center is open daily for hiking, camping, picnicking, bird watching, snow sledding, stargazing or simply enjoying nature.

If skiing is more your style, head down the Lincoln Highway to the Mount Crescent Ski Area. It has been open every year since 1961, when Stein Eriksen, an Olympic gold medalist skier, helped find the perfect spot for a new ski area. Mount Crescent provides beginners to experienced skiers with a variety of slopes. Night skiing is available, thanks to illuminated ski runs.

Through the years, more than 100,000 people have learned how to ski and snowboard at Mount Crescent Ski Area, according to the company's website. When they're not on the slopes, guests often stop by the seven-thousand-square-foot Swiss-inspired lodge at the Mountain Café & Bar.

Nothin' Finer:
Henry's Diner Remains a Crescent Tradition

If skiing in Iowa doesn't interest you, perhaps the tiny town of Crescent will. With a population of roughly seven hundred residents, you almost shake your head in disbelief when you drive in on the Old Lincoln Highway (yes, that's the road's name) and pass not one or two but *four* places to eat, all within half a mile or so. "People always say, 'I can't believe this little town can support all these restaurants,'" said Dale Schmidt of Henry's Diner in Crescent. "There's enough business to go around though."

At one end is the Pink Poodle, one of Iowa's longest-running steakhouses. In business more than sixty-five years, this is one of the few independent, locally owned steakhouses remaining in the Omaha/Council Bluffs metro area. The Pink Poodle has long been known for some of the best prime rib in area, along with seafood, fried chicken and other specialties. If you're expecting glitz, this is not your place. But if you want an exceptional meal (including homemade salad dressing, fresh-baked bread and hearty soups) served with a side of nostalgia in a comfortable, family-friendly atmosphere, you can't go wrong with the Pink Poodle.

On the opposite side of the Old Lincoln Highway is the Crescent Roadhouse Bar & Grill, which offers bike nights in the warmer months, live music, adult beverages and satisfying food. Keep going a bit farther, and you'll see Denny's Place on the other side of the highway. In business since the 1980s, Denny's Place is widely known for its pizza.

Owner Denny Taylo was a good friend of Henry Schmidt, who opened Henry's Diner just down the road at 836 Old Lincoln Highway in 1983. Schmidt was the kind of guy who was rooted in the local area and loved serving his friends and neighbors. Although Schmidt passed away at age seventy-one in 2011, his legacy lives on at Henry's Diner, which is known for its hot beef sandwiches, homemade soup, fried pork tenderloin sandwiches and homemade onion rings. "We don't go skimpy on our portions," said Dale Schmidt, Henry's son, who runs the business with his brother Duane.

In 1998, the Schmidt family built the current restaurant on the same property where their previous restaurant was located. They demolished the old structure, which had been built in 1929. The new restaurant, which was designed with a bar and a spacious dining room, had about twice the square footage of the old restaurant. Go to Henry's Diner today, and you'll see a steady stream of customers from breakfast to lunch to dinner. It's no wonder, since this place is rural Iowa's version of the bar from *Cheers*, where everybody knows your name. If you're a regular, the waitress already knows whether you're a Pepsi person or a coffee drinker. There can be a surprise now and then though. "You guys were throwing me off when you didn't order the chicken," joked one waitress, as she served an older couple their order of spaghetti, French fries and homemade onion rings one afternoon when I stopped by. She placed bowls of soup and baskets of sandwiches on

Left: While only seven hundred people live in Crescent, Iowa, the town boasts four popular restaurants and bars along the Old Lincoln Highway, including the Crescent Roadhouse Bar & Grill, which offers bike nights in the warmer months, live music, food and drinks. *Author's collection.*

Right: Crescent, Iowa, is home to Henry's Diner, a family-owned business known for its friendly service and generous portions of food, from breaded pork tenderloin sandwiches and hand-cut steaks to slow-cooked Crescent Roast Beef. *Author's collection.*

a table nearby, informing those customers, "The cook knew exactly who this was for before he even started filling your order."

This down-home, personal touch guides people who are grounded in farming, food and family. "There are a lot of Century Farms around here," said Dale Schmidt, referring to farms owned by the same family for one hundred years or more. These rural roots are evident throughout the dining room at Henry's Diner, where the wall décor includes pictures of classic John Deere and Farmall tractors, along with an iconic poster of two little boys in striped overalls, boots and trucker caps asking each other, "You been farming long?"

It's a nod to the area's farming culture, where the Schmidt family's story started. When Henry Schmidt was growing up just north of here near

Beebeetown, Iowa, he worked on his family's farm. After he graduated from Beebeetown High School in 1958, Henry served in the U.S. Army and pursued various careers, from auto body repair to construction, but his heart never left rural Iowa.

After all, that's where he learned how to adapt and overcome when life throws a challenge your way. "Dad had a bad eye and couldn't go to war in the Vietnam era, so he became a cook in the army," Dale Schmidt said. Those culinary skills translated well when he opened Henry's Diner in Crescent. "Dad was a big sirloin guy," Dale added. The menu at Henry's Diner still honors this beef heritage through its hand-cut steaks, including Henry's Sirloin (a twelve-ounce cut) and Joyce's Sirloin (a seven-ounce cut), along with ribeyes, prime rib (served Friday and Saturday evenings) and slow-cooked Crescent Roast Beef.

When longtime customers tell Dale and his brother that their father would be proud of them for what Henry's Diner has become today, that means a lot. "We like working together to keep this place going," Dale said. He thinks back to all the practical lessons his dad taught. "Dad always said, 'As long as you work hard, things will be okay,'" said Dale, who puts in sixty to seventy hours per week at work. "He also said, 'If you're leaning, you need to be cleaning.'"

Dale is also quick to give credit to the diner's great team, which includes about ten to twelve part-time and full-time employees. "We wouldn't be where we are today without them."

The staff and customers of Henry's Diner stick together through good times and bad. When massive flooding occurred along the Missouri River in the spring of 2011, local media dubbed this the "billion-dollar disaster." As raging floodwaters closed the interstates and other main roads in the area, some traffic was rerouted through Crescent. "That sparked some people's interest in the Lincoln Highway, which was good," Dale said.

The COVID-19 pandemic of 2020 into 2021 created a new set of challenges. "When we couldn't have people in our dining room, that definitely hurt our business, especially since most people here don't want breakfast to go," Dale said. "We fought through those tough times and stayed open as much as we could."

Folks appreciated this, since Henry's Diner has always been a place where people look forward to spending time with their friends and savoring a good meal and conversation. Long before COVID-19, a group of guys used to stop by Henry's Diner regularly, usually around 10:00 or 11:00 a.m., to play cribbage. "Dad would play sometimes too," Dale said. "They had a lot of fun for a lot of years."

While many of those older gentlemen have since passed away, this spirit of camaraderie lives on at Henry's Diner. It appeals not only to locals but also customers from the Omaha/Council Bluffs area and Lincoln Highway travelers. "We owe a lot to our customers who have stayed loyal to us," Dale said.

PINK POODLE PLEASES PRIME RIB LOVERS FOR DECADES

As you cruise along the Old Lincoln Highway through Crescent, do check out the Pink Poodle just down the way from Henry's Diner. The Pink Poodle is one of those classic places where people have gathered for generations to enjoy great steaks, satisfying seafood and distinctive sides like the homemade ham and bean soup, fresh-baked loaves of bread and crisp lettuce salads with the house dressing.

You feel like you're stepping into an old-school supper club (the kind with plenty of quirky, local flair) when you walk through the front door. As your eyes adjust to the dim lighting, you might notice the three player pianos off to your left, not far from a sizeable doll collection in a glass case. Walk into the dining area and you might notice a large collection of ceramic and stuffed pink poodles on a counter.

The Pink Poodle was built in the 1940s, originally as a house with a bar. It was transformed into a restaurant in the 1950s. Some say it's called the Pink Poodle because the owner's wife raised apricot poodles. That's not true, said Donna Malone, eighty-three, and she should know. She has worked at the Pink Poodle since Mother's Day 1955, back when Jake Brummer, a friend of her family, was running the place.

Brummer, who had also run the Aeroplane Inn in Honey Creek, bought the Black Glove (formerly Peppy's Place) at 633 Old Lincoln Highway and gave the restaurant a new name. "Jake and his wife went to California when her mother was sick," said Donna, who grew up on a farm near Honey Creek. "After her mother was feeling better, the Brummers returned to Iowa, and Jake had two ideas for the name of his restaurant—the Pink Poodle, or the Purple Onion. They went with Pink Poodle."

Donna started out as a cashier and hostess at the Pink Poodle. One night, Brummer asked her to fill in as a waitress. With her characteristic "can do" attitude, she found that she liked waiting on tables, noted the article "Still Taking Orders," a feature story on Donna that ran in the September/ October 2015 issue of *60 Plus in Omaha*. "Back then, if you got a quarter

Donna Malone (shown here in March 2022) has worked at the Pink Poodle in Crescent since Mother's Day 1955. As one of Iowa's longest-running steakhouses, the Pink Poodle has retained its old-school charm and small-town hospitality and serves what some people consider the best prime rib in a four-state area. *Author's collection.*

per person per table, it was a heck of a tip," said Donna, one of the locals who've carried on the Pink Poodle's heritage. "One Saturday night, I remember making $32. The other girls just couldn't believe it—absolutely unreal. Of course, a lobster dinner back then was $7.95."

Donna also remembers how vital the Lincoln Highway was to the area in those days. "Before Interstate 29 was built in the late 1950s and 1960s, the Lincoln Highway was busier than busy. Sometimes there were so many trucks and cars going by that you'd have to wait a long time to cross the road."

Business at the Pink Poodle hummed along until 1972, when a wayward lit cigarette ignited a fire that destroyed the place. The restaurant was rebuilt by 1975, with distinctive wooden arches salvaged from a building in Omaha that had been ravaged recently by a tornado.

Around this time, Donna kept working in the Crescent area and ran into Kenny Malone, a truck driver she had met years earlier. They married in 1974. She even got a license so she could drive the truck, if needed. It wasn't a big leap for Donna, who had acquired her pilot's license shortly after graduating from Missouri Valley High School. "My brother and I bought a plane, which was a lot of fun," she said.

A woman of many talents, Donna has worked for years as a legal secretary with Jerry Ortman, an attorney in Omaha. Most people know her best, however, as a fixture at the Pink Poodle. As one of Iowa's longest-running steakhouses, the Pink Poodle has retained its old-school charm, small-town hospitality and classic American recipes. It serves what some people consider the best prime rib in a four-state area.

"We're not really fancy, but we have good food," said Donna, whose customers include grandparents who first started coming to the Pink Poodle when they were children. With ties like that, Donna has no plans to retire. "I like my job. I don't want to sit around at home."

Local Lincoln Highway heritage inspired Mark Naughton (shown here in March 2022) to paint his own tribute to the historic route on his shed, which is located along the Lincoln Highway between Crescent and Council Bluffs. *Author's collection.*

Pizza King Serves Up the American Dream

When you travel the Lincoln Highway in Iowa, do leave room for serendipity—those times when you find something good unexpectedly. You'll savor it at Christy Creme (2853 North Broadway), a neighborhood mom and pop ice cream shop along the Lincoln Highway that has served Council Bluffs since 1954 and is known for its sherbet.

Serendipity is also how I discovered Pizza King in Council Bluffs, down the road from Christy Creme. I'm ashamed to admit that I'd driven by Pizza King a number of times before and never noticed it. When I was at the Council Bluffs Public Library in March 2022 to speak about my *Culinary History of Iowa* book, everyone agreed that I should stop at Pizza King to get a bite to eat before I left town. "No, not tonight," I said, thinking it would just be easier to go through a fast-food drive-thru and hit the road for the two-hour drive home.

After all, it was nearly 9:00 p.m. But still…what if this Pizza King place was good? I pulled out my smartphone, checked the map for 1101 North Broadway and saw that it was close by, plus it was open until 10:00 p.m. I asked my mom what she thought, since she was riding along. "Sure, why not?" Pizza King, here we come!

When we walked in the door, it felt more like a steakhouse/Italian restaurant than a pizza joint. The menu was equally interesting, with everything from steaks and sandwiches to lasagna and pizza. The pizzas aren't limited to the standard flavors you typically find in the Midwest. Pizza King offers the Athenian Delight, a flat-crust pizza topped with gyro meat, tomatoes, onions, black olives and feta cheese. Then there's the Greek Cowboy, which is like the Athenian Delight, only it's spiced up with jalapeños, pepperoncini and barbecue sauce. Do save room for dessert, too, since you can choose from a variety of homemade cakes, baklava and more.

I ordered the lasagna, which came with a side of bread and a dish of green beans. I learned fast that Pizza King is known for generous portions. After one bite, I was convinced this was the best lasagna I'd ever had. As we enjoyed our meal, I noticed a gentleman keeping watch now and then over the dining room, even though we were about the only customers left by this time of night.

It turns out that was Dan Poulos, who has run the place with his wife, Kathy (who was also buzzing around the restaurant that night), for more than fifty years. Attention to detail and exceptional customer service have helped Pizza King thrive for decades. The Poulos family is a classic example of how ambition, hard work and grit can still help you achieve the American dream. "We've accomplished a lot of things," Kathy said.

Nothing was given to the Poulos family. Dan was orphaned at a young age when his parents died, and he was raised by aunt. He came to Council Bluffs at age ten. When he was in high school, he and his buddies would go to a restaurant in Omaha that served a tasty new food called pizza.

After graduating in 1959 from Abraham Lincoln High School, Poulos served in the U.S. Army before returning to Council Bluffs. Along the way, Poulos had noticed that pizza was really becoming a thing in many of the areas he'd visited. In 1965, he and his younger brother, Pete, decided they wanted a slice of this business and opened Pizza King on Broadway in Council Bluffs.

After Dan married Kathy, a fellow Greek immigrant, in 1966, she, too, helped Pizza King grow. But something beyond the family's control soon threatened the future of their young restaurant. "That area had the misfortune of being part of the 'Super Block,' Phase 1 of Council Bluffs' aggressive urban renewal program," noted retired dentist Richard Warner, who is now a podcast host and local history writer with the Historical Society of Pottawattamie County. "This razed 109 buildings in 1973 in the heart of downtown to make way for a downtown shopping center."

Dan and Kathy Poulos and their family have owned and operated the popular Pizza King restaurant in Council Bluffs for more than fifty years. The spacious restaurant and lounge combines a steakhouse, Italian restaurant and pizza place all in one and is known for exceptional food and excellent service. *Author's collection.*

The plan was designed to save downtown Council Bluffs from the suburban sprawl that was killing other downtowns across the country, but it didn't work. "Many of the local businesses that were displaced chose not to move and reopen, but fortunately Pizza King did," Warner said.

Around this time, another big change worked in Pizza King's favor. The reroute of U.S. Highway 6 claimed the former St. Patrick's School in Council Bluffs, but the school's newer addition was spared, and Pizza King moved in. The business thrived and became a local landmark in the process. In September 2015, Pizza King celebrated fifty years in business. The *Council Bluffs Nonpareil* reported that Mayor Matt Walsh signed a proclamation officially declaring September 21 as Pizza King Day in Council Bluffs.

Today, the restaurant is open seven nights a week (except Christmas and Easter) and features a full-service lounge and party room. Every day, at least one of member of the Poulos family is at the restaurant, including Pete's son Christopher and Dan and Kathy's son George and their daughter, Helen, who helps part time. They still mourn the loss of their son Danny Jr., who died in 2013 at age forty-two from a brain tumor. "The hardest thing was losing our son, who was in the business with us," Dan said.

No matter what, the Poulos family has always tackled the hard times together. "We're a very strong family," Kathy said. When the COVID-19 pandemic hit the country hard in 2020, carryout orders saved Pizza King after mandatory lockdowns shut down the dining room for eighty-two days.

The Poulos family is grateful for all their loyal employees (including forty-seven full-time and part-time team members) and great friends they've met through Pizza King. "We like the people," said Dan, who used to work about eighty hours a week but has cut back to around fifty.

Kathy agreed, adding that she and Dan feel healthy and have no plans to retire anytime soon. "We can't just stay home and look at the walls! We'll keep working. The people here are so good."

UNIQUE HOMES SHARE COUNCIL BLUFFS' HISTORY

When you're in Council Bluffs, there are plenty of interesting places to check out. If you like Victorian homes, tour the Dodge House, a National Historic Landmark. Grenville Dodge, a Union army officer, built his fourteen-room mansion (complete with a ballroom on the third floor) in 1869. Located at 605 South Third Street, the house was designed by William Boyington, a Chicago architect. It cost of $35,000, a lavish sum for the day (the equivalent of more than $730,000 in 2022 dollars).

The Dodge House helped bring some refinement to what was essentially the frontier. It's interesting to note that Dodge met Abraham Lincoln by chance in Council Bluffs in 1859. Dodge, a young engineer, reassured the future president that the Platte Valley would one day be the route of the Pacific Railroad (now known as the transcontinental railroad). In less than a decade, Dodge would become the chief engineer of that project. (The Lincoln Monument, which has stood in Lincoln Monument Park on Lafayette Avenue in Council Bluffs since 1911, commemorates Lincoln's visit to this area in 1859. From this site, Lincoln selected the eastern terminus of the transcontinental railroad.)

Speaking of railroads and historic homes, take a tour of the Union Pacific Railroad Museum at 200 Pearl Street in Council Bluffs. Also, don't overlook the Bregant Home, a little house with a big history. Completed in 1912, this home at 517 Fourth Street once belonged to Jean and Inez (Lewis) Bregant and was custom-built to fit their unique needs. Jean and Inez Bregant, who married in 1905, were known as "the little people" by local residents. Jean stood about forty-five inches tall, while Inez was about forty-two inches tall.

The Bregants met while performing together in a vaudeville troupe at Coney Island, New York. When they lived in Council Bluffs, they met John Woodward, owner of the John G. Woodward and Company candy factory. "Local lore has it John G. Woodward invented and patented the

MR. AND MRS. JEAN BREGANT
SELLING
Woodward's
Pure Sugar Stick Candy and Real Butter Scotch
MADE BY JOHN G. WOODWARD & CO.
"THE CANDY MEN"
COUNCIL BLUFFS, IOWA

Above: A National Historic Landmark, this striking Council Bluffs home was built in 1869 by Grenville Dodge, a Union army officer and acquaintance of Abraham Lincoln who helped guide the construction of America's transcontinental railroad. Dodge's fourteen-room mansion includes a ballroom on the third floor and is open to the public for tours. *Author's collection.*

Left: Jean and Inez (Lewis) Bregant of Council Bluffs lived in a tiny, custom-designed Craftsman bungalow home that was completed in 1912 and is located at 517 Fourth Street. Jean stood about forty-five inches tall, while Inez was about forty-two inches tall. John G. Woodward hired the couple to represent his candy company. The "Candy Kids" traveled to many states, selling Woodward Candy and handing out advertising postcards like this one, circa 1913. *Author's collection.*

flavor butter brickle," said Richard Warner with the Historical Society of Pottawattamie County.

Woodward hired Jean and Inez to represent his company. For seven years, they traveled across many states, demonstrating and selling Woodward Candy and handing out advertising postcards featuring their likeness and the Woodward brand.

DO SOME TIME AT THE SQUIRREL CAGE JAIL

While Jean and Inez were traveling the country, probably on the Lincoln Highway at times, other people stuck close to Council Bluffs, especially if they were incarcerated at the Squirrel Cage Jail on Pearl Street. Today, about six thousand to eight thousand people per year (including some former inmates) visit the three-story rotary jail that opened in 1885, noted Kat Slaughter, manager of the Squirrel Cage Jail, which is now a museum.

In the early 1880s, Pottawattamie County officials had assessed options for a new jail—one that would be durable and difficult to escape. Crime was on the rise in this era, noted S.M. Senden, author of the book *Squirrel Cage Jail*. Outlaw gangs led by the likes of Jesse James and other tough criminals were terrorizing parts of the Midwest, including Iowa. More communities, including Maryville, Missouri, were installing new rotary jails, an innovative design patented by William Brown and Benjamin Haugh of Indianapolis, Indiana, in 1881.

Cells in these rotary jails were shaped like pie slice wedges on a platform that rotated in a carousel fashion. The surrounding of the entire level had a single opening, allowing only one cell at a time to be accessible. One of the main selling points for this unique style of jail was that one man could turn the entire cell drum using a large hand crank. This was considered a safe, secure design that could help save manpower and make the operation of the jail more affordable.

In February 1884, the Pottawattamie County Board of Supervisors agreed to build a three-story rotary jail in Council Bluffs. Not everyone was pleased. Some locals accused members of the Pottawattamie County Board of Supervisors of being too cheap to build a conventional jail. Others called this new jail "Hotel de Guittar" after the current sheriff, Theodore Guittar.

Nevertheless, construction began, and Pottawattamie County built the jail for $28,350 (nearly $830,000 in 2022 dollars). "Compared to other building options, this was a vast savings for the county," Senden wrote.

By the time the Squirrel Cage was complete, the exterior of the jail looked more like a Victorian carriage house than a fortress-style institution, which defined most prisons of that era. On September 10, 1885, Pottawattamie County transferred fifteen prisoners from the old courthouse jail to the Squirrel Cage Jail.

About eighteen rotary jails were built across the country in the 1880s. Today, only three remain. All are museums, including the one-story rotary jail in Gallatin, Missouri; a two-story rotary jail (which can still rotate) in Crawfordsville, Indiana; and the three-story Squirrel Cage Jail in Council Bluffs, the largest rotary jail built in America.

The Squirrel Cage's jail cylinder measures twenty-eight feet high and twenty-four feet in diameter. It weighs ninety thousand pounds empty. There are ten cells per floor, for a total of thirty cells. The Squirrel Cage has three floors of cells, and all the floors would rotate as one solid piece. There was only one opening on each floor. This design gave the jailer as much control as possible. The jailer could crank the cells around to reach a specific inmate or to place an inmate in a cell.

Each cell was about eight feet high and seven and a half feet deep at the center. Each cell could hold two prisoners and included bunk beds and a

The Squirrel Cage, complete with a three-story rotary jail, has been located on Pearl Street in downtown Council Bluffs since 1885. While the jail closed permanently in 1969, it's now a museum. Roughly six thousand to eight thousand people (including some former inmates) tour the property each year. *Author's collection.*

built-in toilet, which was quite remarkable considering the time when the jail was built.

Under normal conditions, the rotating jail cell unit in the Squirrel Cage had a capacity of 60 inmates. However, during the 1932 Farmers' Holiday Strike, 55 to 165 men were held in the Squirrel Cage for a short time, Senden noted. "This large number of incarcerated men was unprecedented and never repeated. For the majority of the jail's history, an average of about 25 to 30 prisoners were housed at any given time."

So, why were farmers revolting in the summer of 1932? While the 1929 stock market crash plunged America into the Great Depression, American farmers had been struggling through an even longer financial depression that started in the early 1920s. After World War I ended, export markets diminished, which led to a chain of events that caused farm commodity prices to decline and farmland values to crash. The onset of the Great Depression only compounded farmers' problems.

Crop prices in 1932 were less than a third of what they had been in 1920—so low that farmers were paying more to produce their crops than they earned from selling them, according to the article "Farmers Holiday Strike of 1932" on the Council Bluffs Public Library's website.

A farmer leader name Milo Reno decided to take direct, radical action. Forming a protest movement known as the Farmers' Holiday Association, Reno encouraged farmers to stop selling and buying, since he believed that withholding crops, milk and more from the market would draw attention to the farmers' plight. "We'll eat our wheat and ham and eggs," Reno said, "and let them eat their gold."

Farmers' Holiday meetings were held in Council Bluffs, Clarinda and other Iowa towns. The Lincoln Highway town of Logan was among the first communities in western Iowa to strike, with picketers lining the roads.

As the protests gained momentum across the state, hundreds of farmers from five Iowa counties met in the Lincoln Highway town of Dunlap on August 22, 1932, to discuss plans to picket roads leading to Omaha. Within days, four hundred farmers met at the fairgrounds in another Lincoln Highway town, Missouri Valley, where a 90 percent majority voted to picket highways leading into Council Bluffs.

Farmer Jim Hawn of Woodbine said, "I'm over 60 years of age, and I've lost everything but my tongue, but I'm sure going out and use it." The farmers met with local law enforcement to announce their intentions and promised their protest would be orderly and peaceful.

In late August, farmers began picketing on highways leading into Council Bluffs. Pottawattamie County sheriff Percy Lainson warned the group that they would not be allowed to block traffic. Carrying signs and shouting slogans, some picketers began placing timbers on the highway to block trucks from delivering to markets in Council Bluffs. Calling the farmers "hoodlums," Sheriff Lainson said, "They have thrown down the gauntlet... and I'm going to fight it out if it takes 5,000 deputies. If the Pottawattamie County jail bulges with pickets, it will have to bulge."

Undeterred, the group began knocking down telephone poles to block produce trucks. The sheriff moved quickly to swear in ninety-eight special deputies, arming each with a club.

In Council Bluffs, forty-nine picketers were arrested and jailed. The mood was tense as two hundred farmers resumed picketing on August 25. Sheriff Lainson upgraded the arsenal of the special deputies, trading their clubs for riot guns and submachine guns. It was reported that a group of one thousand farmers was traveling south to Council Bluffs to aid the picketers and to break arrested farmers out of the Squirrel Cage Jail. While training with their new riot guns, two special deputies were shot accidentally. One, Claude Dail of Council Bluffs, a World War I veteran who had only been a deputy for three days, died within two hours from his wounds.

Within days, the number of protesting farmers swelled to 1,500 at Highway 34 alone. As the caravan of an estimated 1,000 farmers approached Council Bluffs to storm the Squirrel Cage Jail, the chamber of commerce called for an emergency "peace conference." Council Bluffs' mayor, the police chief and the sheriff met at the Hotel Chieftain with a delegation of striking farmers. The meeting was a success by all accounts. After three and half hours of negotiations, the farmers offered to withdraw 90 percent of the group if the sheriff would support a small group of peaceful protesters.

After days of increasingly intense standoffs, tensions seemed to ease. Within a short amount of time, a group of farmers and their supporters managed to raise $5,000 to bail the incarcerated farmers from jail. While the Farmers' Holiday failed to achieve many of its stated goals, it did pressure officials to take action. Nine months after the protests in Council Bluffs, Congress passed the first farm bill as part of President Franklin Roosevelt's New Deal. This Agricultural Adjustment Act launched a program to raise agricultural prices by paying farmers to limit production.

Is the Squirrel Cage Jail Haunted?

Apart from unique cases like the Farmers' Holiday movement, most of the inmates housed at the Squirrel Cage through the years were petty criminals who served time for vagrancy, breaking and entering, burglary, forgery, drunkenness, reckless driving or embezzlement. There were others, however, who committed much more serious crimes, including assault, kidnapping and murder.

Perhaps the most notorious was Jake Bird, a transient serial killer who murdered at least forty-four people across America, typically using the blunt end of an axe, Senden noted. Bird was arrested and tried for the attempted murder of Harold Stribling of Carter Lake, Iowa, on November 20, 1928, after Bird had killed three other people in the area. He was found guilty and sentenced to thirty years at Iowa's Fort Madison State Penitentiary.

Bird was freed from Fort Madison, however, in 1941, for good behavior and time earned. Once out of prison, Bird continued to rob and murder people across the United States. In 1947, a jury in Washington State convicted him of using an axe to kill two women. Bird was sentenced to death and hanged at the Washington State Penitentiary in Walla Walla, Washington, in October 1949. Before he died, he cursed those who were involved in his trial, placing a hex on anyone who had anything to do with his case.

While Bird is long gone, his infamy lives on, due in part to shows like *Ghost Adventures* on the Travel Channel. The *Ghost Adventures* crew traveled to the Squirrel Cage to film footage for the episode "Serial Killer Spirits: Axe Killer Jail," which first aired in October 2019. "*Ghost Adventures* was incredibly professional and very fun to work with," said Slaughter, who has heard mysterious footsteps, doors opening, unexplained whistling and an 1800s-era vintage music box play on its own in the jail. Sometimes these things happen in the day, sometimes they occur at night and sometimes they happen when she's the only one in the building.

While it's hard to explain those odd occurrences, one thing is clear: the Squirrel Cage required major changes by the 1960s. After decades of daily use, the rotary cells were getting stuck. Inmates were getting injured because of this, and access to food and water also became an issue when the Squirrel Cage stopped rotating in 1960. The fire marshal required that changes be made.

After modifications were completed, Pottawattamie County continued to use the Squirrel Cage for nine more years, before the jail finally closed permanently in 1969. After the Squirrel Cage Jail closed, the Council Bluffs'

Cells at the Squirrel Cage in Council Bluffs are shaped like pie-slice wedges on a platform that rotated in a carousel fashion. Some say the Squirrel Cage Jail (shown here 2020) is haunted. *Author's collection.*

Park Board acquired it in 1971, and the jail was placed in the National Register of Historic Places in 1972. By 1977, the Historical Society of Pottawattamie County was leading efforts to preserve the jail. This group owns and operates the facility today.

Perhaps one of the most unique perspectives you can get on the Squirrel Cage Jail comes from Jason "JW" LeMaster, a sergeant of the civil/records division for the Pottawattamie County Sheriff's Office. LeMaster, a former Omaha police officer who has worked in public safety his whole career, is also a longtime volunteer with the Historical Society of Pottawattamie County, where he has served as vice-president of the board since 2016.

I was interested in his take not only on the jail's history but also on the alleged hauntings. Full disclosure here: I have visited the Squirrel Cage Jail a few times, first as a tourist during the day and then as a ghost hunter at night in February 2020, where we had access to all levels of the jail, from the first floor to the apartment at the top. While I didn't experience anything out of the ordinary, I know that many others have had paranormal encounters in the jail. I wanted to see what LeMaster has to say about all this, so I interviewed him in March 2022:

As a law enforcement officer, what interests you about the Squirrel Cage Jail?

I've always been fascinated with history. When I returned to Pottawattamie County as a deputy, I wanted to help preserve the history of the Sheriff's Office. I found that there wasn't much information out there, but the Squirrel Cage Jail did have a few items.

Also, when the Squirrel Cage Jail was in the process of becoming a museum in the 1970s, they held various fundraising events, including "arresting" prominent people in town and having them come to the jail and make phone calls to get bail. (Actually, it was to see if they could get people to donate money for the fake arrest for a good cause). My grandfather Bart Ruby worked at city hall at the time, and they asked him if he would be willing to be "arrested" for the fundraiser. He was more than willing to help. Once I heard this story, my love for the Squirrel Cage Jail grew stronger.

There are a lot of skeptics when it comes to the paranormal, but it seems something is active at the Squirrel Cage Jail. What do you think?

I grew up in a house where my mother always talked about a spirit that lived there. We would have odd things happen, and she would always say that our ghost "Fred" was causing it.

When I would do work at the Squirrel Cage and would be there late at night by myself, I would always announce, "Hey guys, it's just me," when I walked in. I never had anyone answer me back. When I left, I'd announce, "Alright guys, I'm leaving. I'll see you next time."

One night I was notified that a light was left on in the upstairs bathroom of the Squirrel Cage Jail, so my wife, Kim, and I stopped by to turn off the light. Kim is an analytical person. In her mind, if something strange happens, there's an obvious reason for it. While we were there, out of the blue there was a loud noise. It sounded like something very large made out of wood being dropped onto a wood floor. We both turned and looked to see what it was. We went to find what had obviously fallen and found nothing. *There was no reason for the noise.*

Kim then said that it was time to go and announced, "Ok guys, we're leaving now." This made me laugh because she had no clue that I would sometimes say this as I was leaving. To this day, she still talks about this incident whenever anyone asks if she has seen or heard anything happening in the jail.

There's so much history at this unique jail. What stands out to you?

We're learning more stories each day. I'm scanning in old arrest records at the Sheriff's Office, including ones from the time that the Squirrel Cage Jail was used. I'm finding stories of assaults that took place inside the building, escapes that have been forgotten over time and all kinds of crazy things that would otherwise have been lost if someone wouldn't have seen the records again.

The other thing that amazes me is the number of people who have been incarcerated there through the years. We're seen some of these the names written and scribbled on the walls and ceiling and tables. Now we're finding more names. I'm also finding the mug shots (I have almost three thousand to date), so now we're seeing the faces behind those names. There are adults and teenagers of every race and gender now staring back at us from the mug shots, which date from the 1940s to 1969. It gives you chills to see what's behind the eyes of some of these people. This is history staring back at us from afar.

Anything else you'd like to add about the Squirrel Cage Jail?

Once history is lost, it's gone forever. We're trying to preserve it the best we can at the Squirrel Cage Jail, and we could always use help. If you're local, come visit. If you're from out of town, come visit. We love telling the story of the jail. Proceeds from tours and fundraisers help us preserve the artifacts we currently have and help us acquire more to help tell the story of days gone by. Stop by for a tour, learn some history and have some fun! Who knows? Maybe a spirit will reach out to talk to you while you're here.

THE LINCOLN HIGHWAY
ROLLS ON

S o here we are, having toured the Lincoln Highway from river to river in Iowa. If you feel so inclined, you can become an official member of the Lincoln Highway Association like me and hundreds of other people who love the Lincoln Highway, an enduring symbol of freedom, patriotism and America's adventurous spirit.

The Lincoln Highway appeals not only to Americans but also travelers around the globe. "It's not unusual for Europeans, Japanese and other world travelers to come to the United States for a cross-country road trip on the Lincoln Highway," said Drake Hokanson, author of *The Lincoln Highway: Main Street Across America*, when I visited with him. "They sense the significance of the American road trip, which is an iconic part of American culture."

Iowa remains a huge part of this Lincoln Highway heritage. "When I started my research in the 1980s into the Lincoln Highway, there was a stronger memory of the highway in Iowa than in other states," said Hokanson, a photographer, author, editor and former University of Iowa instructor who now lives in Wisconsin. "Iowa paid attention to the Lincoln Highway more than states like Utah, Nevada or Pennsylvania."

Iowa is often considered the pinnacle of touring the Lincoln Highway, added Brian Butko, author of the book *Greetings from the Lincoln Highway: A Road Trip Celebration of America's First Coast-to-Coast Highway*. "There are lots of small towns to explore, intertwined generations of the route to drive, numerous historic bridges, helpful signage to follow the road, and a great balance of rural views, while never being too far between things to see."

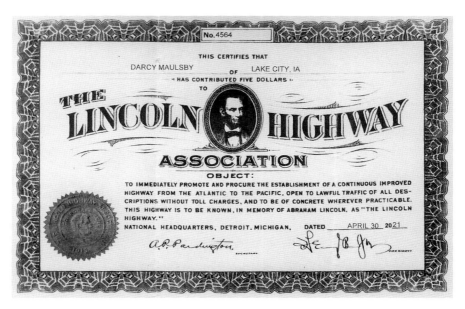

For a modest fee, you can become a member of the National Lincoln Highway Association, which is dedicated to preserving and celebrating this important part of American history. *Author's collection.*

LINCOLN HIGHWAY OFFERS A "NIFTY ALTERNATIVE"

If you're looking for some road trip music when you're traveling the Lincoln Highway in Iowa, tune into Shadric Smith, who wrote an ode to the Lincoln Highway in 1995. "Ken put a bug in my ear about writing a song about the Lincoln Highway," said Smith, referring to his friend Ken Huffaker of Nevada, Iowa. Ken owned the Nevada Monument Company (located along the old Lincoln Highway) and was active with the Story County town's annual Lincoln Highway Days festival.

Smith—a skilled musician, folksinger and longtime Fort Dodge resident—thought that the project sounded interesting. He read a book to brush up on his knowledge of the Lincoln Highway. "The story of the Lincoln Highway is remarkable," said Smith, a singer-songwriter who lived in Nashville, Tennessee, for a time. "What we take for granted today with road transportation goes back to the development of the Lincoln Highway."

The challenges that faced the Lincoln Highway's founders, as well as early motorists, resonated with Smith. "In the beginning, the Lincoln Highway was dirt and would turn to mud when it rained. Then you'd have to dig out of the muck. Those people who set out to travel the Lincoln Highway years ago were pretty brave."

As he wrote "Rollin' Down that Lincoln Highway," Smith wanted to convey the can-do spirit of progress and freedom that defines the highway. He also thought of his own connections to the Lincoln Highway. He worked for Rieman Music's Fort Dodge location for eighteen years, starting in the mid-1990s. "I had a route of about forty-five schools in the area, and Friday was the day that took me to the Lincoln Highway," said Smith, who sold musical instruments and taught guitar lessons. "I always liked traveling on the Lincoln Highway between Jefferson and Scranton. You can still see traces of the old highway's history in this area."

Iowa's portion of the Lincoln Highway has much to offer, wrote Michael Wallis in *The Lincoln Highway: The Great American Road Trip.* "Some of the best of the Lincoln is in this state—running through farmland and fields and the many towns and cities the highway either skirts or passes through. It is an ideal state for nostalgia buffs to rediscover the hidden charms of the Lincoln Highway." *Author's collection.*

It took Smith a few hours to write "Rollin' Down that Lincoln Highway." When he first recorded the song in 1996 in Otho, Iowa, he played guitar and sang on the recording and then overdubbed the bass and organ parts. Huffaker used the recording at several Lincoln Highway events in Nevada. That same year, the song was used in a promotional video for the Lincoln Highway shot by Roger Riley from the Iowa Lincoln Highway Association.

"I like the idea of sharing the history of the Lincoln Highway and helping people understand its importance," said Smith, who has performed at many venues and town celebrations around Iowa with the Frontier Fiddle Band.

In 2003, Smith recorded "Rollin' Down that Lincoln Highway" again at Big Blue Sound in Fort Dodge. If you'd like to listen to this catchy, upbeat tune, you can find it online on Spotify, Amazon Music, Apple Music and YouTube. It's worth a listen, especially for your next road trip.

"Even though interstates make travel faster and easier today, the Lincoln Highway still provides a nifty alternative, especially if you want to see Iowa's small towns," Smith said. "Traveling on a two-lane road like the Lincoln Highway is more relaxing, too, than flying down the interstate."

"ROLLIN' DOWN THAT LINCOLN HIGHWAY"
Rollin' down that Lincoln Highway
The oldest road from shore to shore
Built way back when by those hard-workin' men
They had a dream, but they still wanted more.

So from New York City to the Frisco Bay
The pavement never ever stops.
It's like Main Street…across the USA
With truckers, businessmen and traffic cops…

CHORUS
I'm rollin' down that Lincoln Highway
Rollin' down that Lincoln Highway
Rollin' down that Lincoln Highway
Rollin' down that Lincoln Highway

LINCOLN HIGHWAY NAMED NATIONAL SCENIC BYWAY

Some say that Interstate 80 is the road the Lincoln Highway was intended to be. Still, if you only travel on interstates, rushing by farms and towns along the way, you'll often miss what Hokanson calls the "grand montage of detail" that transforms a remote abstraction into a vivid impression of a trip, a state, a country.

Granted, it's difficult sometimes to spot the Lincoln Highway's heritage in larger communities along the route. "In such places, the city dominates the highway into submission," Hokanson wrote. "If the Lincoln is to be found at all, it will be in the countryside."

Iowa's portion of the Lincoln Highway has much to offer, wrote Michael Wallis in *The Lincoln Highway: The Great American Road Trip.* "Some of the best of the Lincoln is in this state—running through farmland and fields and the many towns and cities the highway either skirts or passes through. It is an ideal state for nostalgia buffs to rediscover the hidden charms of the Lincoln Highway."

Joshua Hopkins understands this well. In an essay called "A Cowboy Heads Home for Christmas on the Lincoln Highway," he detailed his December 2020 journey along the Lincoln Highway from Wyoming to Pennsylvania. He was especially impressed with Iowa, as he noted in the essay, which appeared in the spring 2021 edition of *Lincoln Highway Forum* magazine.

"Continuing up the road, I was very surprised to find signage for the original highway, even very short meandering stubs of dirt and that it was well marked all across Iowa," wrote Hopkins, describing his journey after enjoying a good "truck-stop dinner meal" in Missouri Valley. "It felt in many ways as if I was traveling as the original motorists did, looking out for the signs…and letting the adventure unfold on its own. Iowa turned out to be my most favorite of states visited, as it seemed to hold the most core American culture spread across a mostly rural state, still reliant on agriculture with many of its small towns intact and necessary lifelines for the farmers themselves. If I had to pick one states that embodies the spirit of the American people other than my state of Wyoming…it would have to be Iowa."

The Lincoln Highway is a route for travelers, not tourists. "Tourists flock to the franchise eateries and the chain motels because they know what to expect," Wallis noted. "Travelers, on the other hand, are more apt to enjoy a cruise on the Lincoln Highway. People who hanker for the hidden places off the well-beaten tourist path will invariably find this remarkable highway much to their liking."

The endless appeal of the Lincoln Highway is that it can mean different things to different people. "During my work with the Lincoln Highway Association in Iowa, I found that interests in the Lincoln Highway could take a number of directions, from historic bridge design to roadside culture and more," said Roger Riley, a photojournalist with WHO-TV in Des Moines.

For some, traveling the Lincoln Highway offers a unique way to honor history. I enjoyed watching about sixty vintage trucks, jeeps and other vehicles drive the Lincoln Highway during the 2019 Military Convoy Centennial Tour. Drivers making the long trek from the East Coast to California retraced the route taken by the U.S. Army convoy during the summer of 1919. When the 100th anniversary convoy came through Greene County on August 24, I joined the crowds lining the sides of the old Lincoln Highway in Grand Junction and waved as members of the Military Vehicle Preservation Association drove by. It was also fun to talk with the drivers when they stopped for a late-afternoon break in Jefferson around the courthouse square.

In August 2019, trucks, jeeps and other military vehicles crossed the Lincoln Highway from coast to coast during the 2019 Military Convoy Centennial Tour, which retraced the route taken by the U.S. Army convoy in 1919. Johnny Rossman of State College, Pennsylvania, posed for photos during a stop in Jefferson, Iowa. *Author's collection.*

No doubt the drivers noticed the Lincoln Highway Heritage Byway signs along the route in Iowa. The Lincoln Highway became part of the Iowa Department of Transportation's Scenic Byway program in 2006. The Lincoln Highway Heritage Byway is Iowa's longest and most historic byway, traveling through more than 460 miles of history, recreation and welcoming Iowa communities.

Another big milestone occurred on February 16, 2021, when the Lincoln Highway Heritage Byway was designated a National Scenic Byway. By some accounts, this puts the Lincoln Highway in Iowa on equal footing with the legendary Route 66. "With this honor, the Iowa section of the Lincoln Highway will continue to gain visibility worldwide," said Prairie Rivers of Iowa executive director Penny Brown Huber.

The Lincoln Highway gained more visibility in the early summer of 2022 thanks to Jack Smith and his electric "Rust Bus." It all started when Smith (who had lived in north-central Iowa for a time in the 1990s) watched the Ken Burns documentary *Horatio's Drive* at his home in Morro Bay, California. Smith was hooked. He bought the companion book for the film and delved further into the story of Horatio Nelson Jackson's 1903 cross-country journey. Then, he decided it wasn't enough for him to simply read about Horatio's drive. "I told my wife, 'I want to retrace this guy's route, but I don't want to do it in a regular vehicle.'"

He wanted an electric vehicle, so he contacted his friend Michael Bream, owner of EV West in San Marcos, California. While Smith was thinking of a Tesla, Bream offered the "Rust Bus," a drafty, 1963 Volkswagen van that he converted to run on electric power.

After driving the Rust Bus from west to east in early May 2022, it was time to head back on the Lincoln Highway. At night, Smith and his buddy Larry Newland stayed at campgrounds. They plugged in the bus to charge overnight,

In May and June 2022, Jack Smith crossed the country from coast to coast in the "Rust Bus," a 1963 Volkswagen van converted to run on electric power. As he headed home to California, he traveled on the Lincoln Highway. "My two favorite things in Iowa were the Lincoln Highway bridge in Tama and Niland's café and gas station [shown here] in Colo," Smith said. *Courtesy of Jack Smith.*

so they were ready to hit the road by morning. They could cover 160 to 200 miles before needing to recharge.

"I loved seeing the old buildings and the countryside along the Lincoln Highway," said Smith, who wrote the script for the 2020 film *New Providence*, a story about the final season of girls' six-on-six high school basketball in Iowa. "My two favorite things in Iowa were the Lincoln Highway bridge in Tama and Niland's café and gas station in Colo."

The six-week Rust Bus tour made a big impression on sixty-five-year-old Smith. "I like adventure, I like to see America and I like the Lincoln Highway. This trip gave me such respect for early adventurers like Horatio Jackson, who made the trip with an open-top car and a compass, without all the technology we have today."

That's the thing about the Lincoln Highway. This route isn't a relic of the past. It reflects a rich heritage, yet it remains a dynamic part of Iowa today. Best of all, the journey continues. "You find so many interesting stories as you peel back the layers of the onion," Hokanson told me. "Traveling the Lincoln Highway in Iowa is a fine little adventure."

I couldn't agree more. Long live the Lincoln Highway!

BIBLIOGRAPHY

Bannister, Megan. *Iowa Supper Clubs*. Charleston, SC: The History Press, 2020.

Barnes, Suzi. *Memories from the House on Silk Stocking Row, Denison, Iowa*. Logan, IA: Perfection Press, 2010.

Butko, Brian. *Greetings from the Lincoln Highway: A Road Trip Celebration of America's First Coast-to-Coast Highway*. Mechanicsburg, PA: Stackpole Books, 2005.

Duncan, Dayton, and Ken Burns. *Horatio's Drive: America's First Road Trip*. New York: Alfred A. Knopf, 2003.

Federal Highway Administration Lincoln Highway Archives. https://www.fhwa.dot.gov/infrastructure/lincoln.cfm.

Fenster, Julie M. *Race of the Century: The Heroic True Story of the 1908 New York to Paris Auto Race*. New York: Crown Publishers, 2005.

Franzwa, Gregory M. *The Lincoln Highway Iowa*. Vol. 1. Tucson, AZ: Patrice Press, 1995.

Hokanson, Drake. *The Lincoln Highway: Main Street Across America*. Iowa City: University of Iowa Press, 1988.

Iowa Department of Transportation Lincoln Highway Archives. https://iowadot.gov/autotrails/lincolnhighway.

Senden, S.M. *Squirrel Cage Jail Council Bluffs, Iowa*. Charleston, SC: Palmetto Publishing Group, 2019.

Wallis, Michael, and Michael S. Williamson. *The Lincoln Highway: The Great American Road Trip*. New York: W.W. Norton & Company, 2007.

ABOUT THE AUTHOR

I f you enjoy true stories well told, you have a lot in common with Darcy Dougherty Maulsby. As Iowa's Storyteller, Darcy believes that anyone who eats has a connection to the things she's most passionate about, including food, farming and history. As a fifth-generation farmer, business owner, author, marketing specialist, historian and speaker, Darcy helps businesses uncover their "wow" stories and share them to inspire people to dream bigger, revitalize their rural communities and change the world for the good, one story at a time. Darcy earned her journalism/communication's degree and master of business administration degree (with a marketing emphasis) from Iowa State University. After working for several companies in the Des Moines area, including the Iowa Farm Bureau Federation and AgWeb.com, she became an entrepreneur, opened her own business and has run her own marketing/communications company, Darcy Maulsby & Company, full time since 2002.

Darcy often writes about the food-to-fork connection for clients like the Iowa Food & Family Project and through her nonfiction books, including *A Culinary History of Iowa*, *Calhoun County*, *Classic Restaurants of Des Moines and Their Recipes*, *Dallas County*, *Iowa Agriculture: A History of Farming, Family and Food* and *Madison County*. An avid home cook, Darcy has cooked with *American Idol* winner/restauranteur Taylor Hicks during the Iowa episode of the national

TV program *State Plate*. She has also been featured on the Iowa State Fair episode of *Bizarre Foods: Delicious Destinations* on the Cooking Channel. In 2022, Smithsonian dubbed her the "chili and cinnamon rolls expert" and has featured her in an online article.

Darcy is proud to be part of a farm family that operates a Century Farm in Calhoun County, Iowa, near Lake City. Darcy enjoys spending time with her family and pets, cooking (especially homemade soups!) and serving as board president of Central School Preservation in Lake City. Visit her at www.darcymaulsby.com.

Este libro utiliza el tipo Aldus, que toma su nombre del vanguardista impresor del Renacimiento italiano, Aldus Manutius. Hermann Zapf diseñó el tipo Aldus para la imprenta Stempel en 1954, como una réplica más ligera y elegante del popular tipo Palatino

Otra gran obra maestra del cine se acabó de imprimir un día de primavera de 2023, en los talleres gráficos de Egedsa Roís de Corella 12-16, nave 1 Sabadell (Barcelona)

Agradecimientos

Peter Gethers siempre ha conseguido que esta obra fuera mejor. Otra gente de Knopf como Morgan Hamilton, Rita Madrigal, John Gall y Anna Knighton también han trabajado duro. Aplausos, por favor.

Los cómics —komix— surgieron del arte y la pericia de Robert Sikoryak. Cada uno de ellos resultó ser un millón de veces mejor de lo que yo había imaginado, así que aquí van mi agradecimiento y admiración.

Ester Newberg es una auténtica fuerza de la naturaleza y una gran aliada. Qué suerte la mía.

Un agradecimiento especial a D. Narasaki por su guía y «buena fortuna». Y a E. A. Hanks por ser tan buen ejemplo de destreza.

Ann Patchett y Ada Calhoun son dos Grandes Maestras campeonas para mí. Las admiro mucho a ambas y estoy en deuda con ellas para siempre.

Estas páginas no existirían de no ser por Nora. Todos pensamos en ella. Mucho. Cada día.

En las paredes, fotografías antiguas de Amos.

A su abuelo, Amos Knight.
Tiene unos cien años.
Está durmiendo.

Continuará...

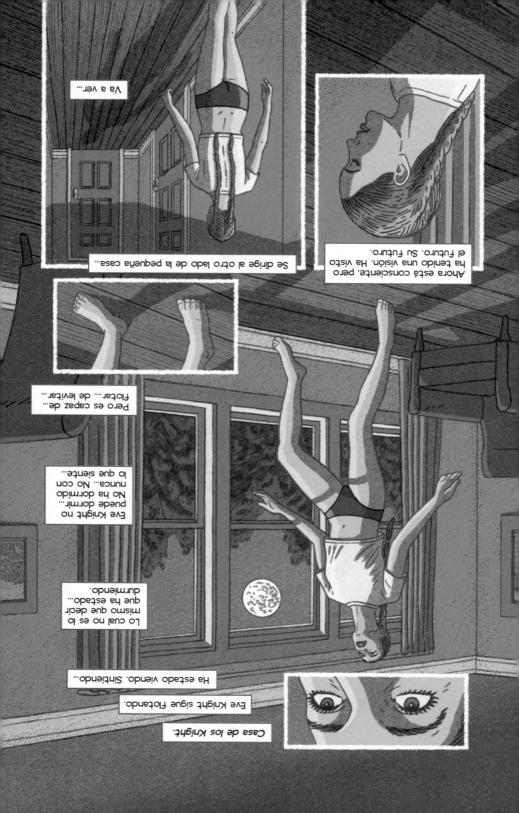

Va a ver...

Ahora está consciente, pero ha tenido una visión. Ha visto el Futuro. Su Futuro.

Se dirige al otro lado de la pequeña casa...

Pero es capaz de... flotar... de levitar...

Eve Knight no puede dormir... No ha dormido nunca... No con lo que siente...

Lo cual no es lo mismo que decir que ha estado... durmiendo.

Ha estado viendo. Sintiendo...

Eve Knight sigue flotando.

Casa de los Knight.

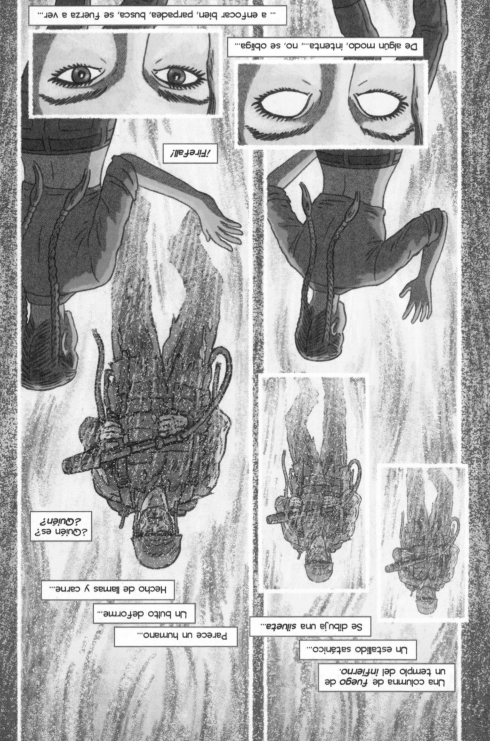

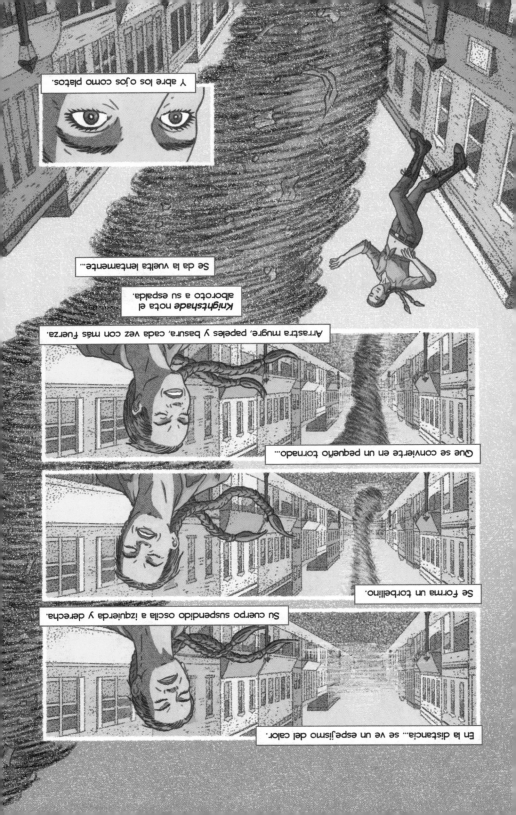

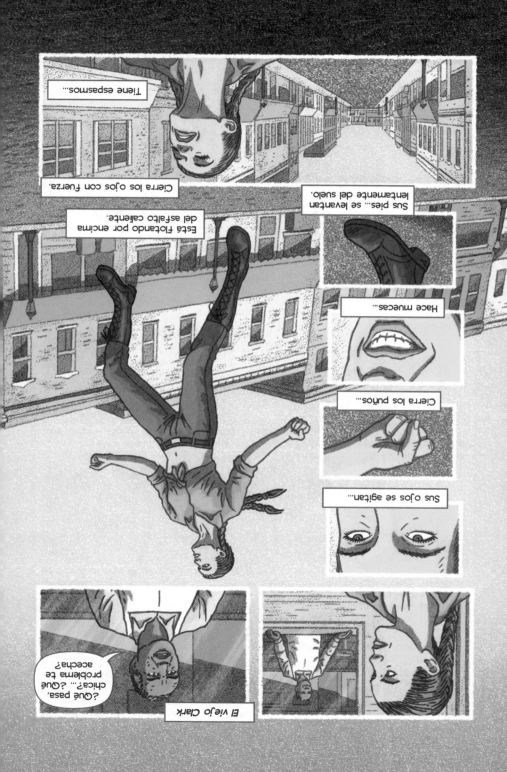

DYNAMO
EDICIÓN
ESPECIAL

KNIGHTSHADE
EL TORNO DE FIREFALL

BASADO EN LA PELÍCULA DE DYNAMO DIRIGIDA POR BILL JOHNSON